VOX,

in a box

SPANISH

Grammar Guide

New York Chicago San Francisco Lisbon London Madrid Mexico City
Milan New Delhi San Juan Seoul Singapore Sydney Toronto

The McGraw·Hill Companies

Copyright © 2011 by Larousse Editorial, S.L. (Barcelona, Spain). All rights reserved.
Printed in the United States of America. Except as permitted under the United States
Copyright Act of 1976, no part of this publication may be reproduced or distributed in
any form or by any means, or stored in a database or retrieval system, without the prior
written permission of the publisher.

1 2 3 4 5 6 7 8 9 10 11 12 13 14 15 16 17   QFR/QFR   1 9 8 7 6 5 4 3 2 1

ISBN 978-0-07-175223-7 (book and CD set)
MHID   0-07-175223-4 (book and CD set)

ISBN 978-0-07-175218-3 (book for set)
MHID   0-07-175218-8 (book for set)

Library of Congress Control Number 2010935995

Editorial director: Jordi Induráin
Edition by: Sofía Acebo
Texts by: Sergi Torner
Translation by: Mark Waudby
Edition assistant: Laura del Barrio
Correction by: Fernando Nápoles
Layout: tresmesú, s. l.

McGraw-Hill books are available at special quantity discounts to use as premiums and
sales promotions or for use in corporate training programs. To contact a representative,
please e-mail us at bulksales@mcgraw-hill.com.

This book is printed on acid-free paper.

Introduction

This *Grammar* is an ideal tool for those students of Spanish as a foreign language who are either beginners (Level A1) or that have previously achieved an intermediate level of knowledge (Level A2).

The brevity of this text is particularly adequate for those who are preparing an exam. On account of its grammatical rigor, it is also very useful for students who, besides a dictionary, also need a reference book that can help them follow their Spanish courses. In either case, analyzing the language they are studying will help both of them to communicate more confidently and skillfully in a language that is not their own.

The contents of this book describe and explain essential Spanish grammatical concepts related to how words are formed; that is, morphology (for example, how verb tenses, noun plurals and comparative adjectives are formed). They also include how words combine to form sentences; that is, syntax (how words in a phrase are ordered to compare two adjectives or two adverbs, or how a question is formed when we want to know who's the subject of the phrase. Although this grammar concentrates essentially on these two aspects, we have also occasionally included some explanations about meanings, pronunciation and orthography.

Contents have been structured in nine chapters related to the main parts of speech in which Spanish words can be classified: nouns, adjectives, articles, pronouns, determiners, verbs, adverbs, prepositions and conjunctions. To simplify explanations, some parts of speech have been discussed on the same chapter, as you can see in the Contents that follows this Introduction. Like English, Spanish has words that belong only to one part of speech (*mesa* is a noun); however, there are other words that might belong to more than one (*solo* functions as an adjective in the phrase: *Siempre jugaba solo* (He always played alone); but it can also function as an adverb like in: *Solo jugaba con sus hermanos* (He only played with his brothers). *Solo* will play a different role in a sentence when it is classified as an adjective or as an adverb.

To make sure that studying Spanish as a foreign language is carried out on a sound base, it is necessary to know and amass many words, although it is also necessary to know how to use them. That is exactly what this grammar will help you to do: to form statements and phrases similar to those of the native speakers of Spanish, to know what they say when they talk and to understand the meaning of the texts they have written.

THE EDITORS

Contents

1. Nouns

In Spanish, all nouns are masculine or feminine and singular or plural.

- The **gender** of a noun helps us to decide whether it is *masculine* or *feminine*. In Spanish, the gender of a noun rarely has any connection with the true gender of the person or animal it refers to.

- The **number** helps us to decide whether the noun is *singular* or *plural*. This distinction is made by the use of the definite articles *el, la* in the singular and *los, las* in the plural, and the indefinite articles *un, una* in the singular and *unos, unas* in the plural.

		GENGER	
		masculine	feminine
NUMBER	singular	el niño *(the boy, the child)*	la niña *(the girl, the child)*
	plural	los niños *(the boys, the children)*	las niñas *(the girls, the children)*

1.1. Gender

In Spanish, all nouns have gender. In other words, they are either masculine or feminine. It is important to know the gender of each noun as the determiners or adjectives that accompany them agree with the noun they modify:

el niño alto *(the tall boy)*   la niña alta *(the tall girl)*

The article that precedes the noun can help us to recognize or remember the gender of the noun: *el libro (the book), la ventana (the window), un hombre (a man), los amigos (the friends), unas fotos (some photos),* etc. This is why, when we learn a new noun, it is important to memorize the noun together with its determiner: *(el) amigo (the friend).*

1. Nouns

Although all nouns have gender, only a few vary according to their gender:

- In Spanish, the masculine gender is used to refer to male people and animals and the female gender refers to female people or animals. The feminine form is made by changing the ending of the masculine noun to −*a*:

el gato / la gata *(the cat)*   el amigo / la amiga *(the friend)*
el presidente / la presidenta *(the president)*   el perro / la perra *(the dog / the bitch)*

- Nouns that designate objects or concepts can be either masculine or feminine:

la mesa *(the table)*   el libro *(the book)*
la amabilidad *(kindness)*   el problema *(the problem)*

A masculine noun (such as *el problema [the problem]*) has no feminine form (you cannot say *la problema*), and a feminine noun (such as *la mesa [the table]*) has no masculine form (you cannot say *el mesa*).

1.1.a. The gender of nouns determined by sex

When the gender of the noun is the same as the actual gender of the person or animal in question, the gender indicates the sex of the person or animal. In these cases, there are four possibilities.

The gender is shown by the ending of the noun

With most nouns, only the vowel at the end changes, or a vowel is added to form the feminine. The feminine form of these nouns always ends in −*a*; the masculine can end in the vowels −*o* and −*e*, or in a consonant:

- masculine -*o* / feminine -*A*

el mono / la mona *(the monkey)*   el niño / la niña *(the boy / the girl)*
el amigo / la amiga *(the friend)*   el gato / la gata *(the cat)*
el abuelo / la abuela   el perro / la perra *(the dog / the bitch)*
  (the grandfather / the grandmother)   el peluquero / la peluquera *(the hairdresser)*
el cocinero / la cocinera *(the cook)*   el primo / la prima *(the cousin)*

- masculine -*CONSONANT* / feminine -*A*

el león / la leona *(the lion / the lioness)*   el marqués / la marquesa
el bailarín / la bailarina *(the dancer)*   *(the marquis / the marquess)*
el señor / la señora *(the man / the woman)*

● masculine -*E* / feminine -*A*

> el presidente / la presidenta *(the president)*   el jefe / la jefa *(the boss)*
> el dependiente / la dependienta *(the salesclerk)*

In some cases, the feminine form takes a completely different ending to the masculine:

> el actor / la actriz *(the actor / the actress)* el rey / la reina *(the king / the queen)*
> el emperador / la emperatriz   el poeta / la poetisa *(the poet)*
>   *(the emperor / the empress)*

The masculine and feminine have completely different forms

There are two different words that are masculine and feminine in gender to refer to the male and female:

> el padre / la madre *(the father / the mother)* el toro / la vaca *(the bull / the cow)*
> el caballo / la yegua *(the horse / the mare)* el macho / la hembra *(the male / the female)*

The same form is used for the masculine and feminine

Although the noun has the same form, its gender varies. In these cases, the gender is shown by the article:

nouns ending in −*NTE*	nouns ending in −*STA*	others
el / la cantante *(the singer)*	el / la pianista *(the pianist)*	el / la cónyuge *(the spouse)*
el / la estudiante *(the student)*	el / la periodista *(the journalist)*	el / la joven *(the young man / the young woman)*

The gender of the noun does not vary

The names of some animals have only one word to refer to the male and female. These noun forms do not vary in gender. In other words, these nouns are always masculine or feminine. The distinction between the sex of the animal is made by adding the word *macho* (male) or *hembra* (female) after the noun.

> el leopardo macho / el leopardo hembra *(the male leopard / the female leopard)*
> la rana macho / la rana hembra *(the male frog / the female frog)*
> la serpiente macho / la serpiente hembra *(the male snake / the female snake)*
> la jirafa macho / la jirafa hembra *(the male giraffe / the female giraffe)*

1.1.b. The expression of gender in nouns not determined by sex

The distinction between masculine and feminine cannot be predicted systematically in the case of nouns that are not determined by sex. This is why, as we have said above, when you learn a new noun, it is important to learn it with its corresponding article. This will help you to remember its gender.

The gender of these nouns is usually arbitrary, meaning that it is not always possible to predict. However, in many cases, these nouns give us a series of clues that can help us deduce the gender. For instance, it can be helpful to look at the *ending* or *word group*.

Gender according to ending

The ending of a noun can give us an idea of its gender.

Masculine nouns usually end in:

-O	el cabello, el olmo, el carro, el libro *(the hair, the elm, the cart, the book)*
-L, -N, -R, -S, -T	el animal, el tren, el solar, el compás, el hábitat *(the animal, the train, the plot of land, the compass, the habitat)*
-ETE	el sorbete, el banquete *(the sorbet, the banquet)*
-OR	el tractor, el color, el colador *(the tractor, the color, the colander)*

Feminine nouns usually end in:

-A	la cabeza, la casa, la mesa, la silla, la cocina *(the head, the house, the table, the chair, the kitchen)*
-IE (s)	la serie, la intemperie, la caries *(the series, the elements, tooth decay)*
-DAD, -IDAD, -TAD	la barbaridad, la soledad, la brutalidad, la libertad *(barbarism, solitude, brutality, freedom)*
-IÓN	la región, la opinión, la religión *(the region, the opinion, religion)*
-TUMBRE, -DUMBRE	la costumbre, la incertidumbre *(the habit, uncertainty)*
-SIÓN, -CIÓN, -ZÓN	la televisión, la canción, la inversión *(the television, the song, the investment)*
-TUD	la exactitud, la virtud, la amplitud *(precision, the virtue, width)*
-TRIZ	la cicatriz *(the scar)*

There are only a few masculine nouns ending in —*a*: *el poema (the poem), el problema (the problem), el teorema (the theorem), el sistema (the system),* etc.

Gender according to specific word groups

The word group a noun belongs to can give us some clues to its gender. The nouns from a specific word group will have the same gender. For instance, *día (day)* is masculine and all the days of the week are masculine; likewise, *letra (letter)* is feminine, and the nouns designating the letters of the alphabet are feminine.

1.2.   Number

In Spanish, the **number,** we should remember, helps us to decide whether the noun is *singular* or *plural.* This distinction is made by the use of the definite articles *el, la* in the singular and *los, las* in the plural, and the indefinite articles *un, una* in the singular and *unos, unas* in the plural.

1.2.a. Forming the plural

In Spanish, the plural is formed by adding -*s* or -*ES* to the singular. The plural endings are determined by the ending of the singular noun.

The general rules for forming the plural are as follows:

Add -*s* to nouns ending in	a non-accented vowel:
	   la casa / las casas *(the house / the houses)*
	   el amigo / los amigos *(the friend / the friends)*

	an accented vowel -*e*:
	   el café / los cafés *(coffee / the coffees;*
	   the café / the cafés)

	an accented vowel other than -*e*:
	   el esquí / los esquís *(the ski / the skis)*
	   el rubí / los rubíes *(the ruby / the rubies)*

Add -*ES* to nouns ending in	a consonant other than -*s*:
	   el camión / los camiones *(the truck / the trucks)*
	   la pared / las paredes *(the wall / the walls)*
	   el tractor / los tractores *(the tractor / the tractors)*

	an accented vowel other than -*e*:
	   el esquí / los esquís *(the ski / the skis)*
	   el rubí / los rubíes *(the ruby / the rubies)*

> an accented vowel followed by -s:
> el país / los países *(the country / the countries)*
> el autobús / autobuses *(the bus / the buses)*

Nouns with the following endings are invariable

> an unstressed vowel followed by -s:
> el atlas / los atlas *(the atlas / the atlases)*
> la tesis / las tesis *(the thesis / the theses)*
> la crisis / las crisis *(the crisis / the crises)*
> el lunes / los lunes *(Monday / Mondays)*

1.2.b. Plural forms

'One' compared with 'more than one'

The meaning of a noun does not normally vary if it is singular or plural. With most concrete nouns, the distinction between singular and plural expresses the opposition between 'one' (with the indefinite article *un, una* in the singular) and 'more than one' (with *varios, varias* meaning 'several' in the plural).

For example: *un coche (a car), varios coches (several cars), un libro (a book), varios libros (several books),* etc. These are the most frequent values of the plural.

Other plural forms

In a few cases, the distinction between singular and plural is not related to the difference between 'one' and 'more than one'. The main plural values in Spanish are as follows:

- Some nouns are usually plural but refer to a single object: *gafas (glasses, spectacles), pantalones (pants), tijeras (scissors)), calzoncillos (underpants), tenazas (pliers),* etc. These are known as non-informative plurals.

- In some cases, the singular and plural forms of the noun have completely different meanings: *esposa (su primera esposa [his first wife])]) / esposas (Le pusieron las esposas y lo llevaron a comisaría. [They handcuffed him and took him to the police station.])*.

- Some nouns that are uncountable in the singular become countable in the plural: *El café es muy aromático. (Coffee is very aromatic.). Se tomó dos cafés. (She had two coffees.)*.

2. Adjectives

Adjectives are words that designate the properties and attributes of the nouns they qualify. In Spanish, adjectives vary with gender and number, just like nouns. However, unlike nouns, they have no intrinsic gender or number. In other words, adjectives always have the same gender and number as the noun they qualify.

		GENDER	
		masculine	feminine
NUMBER	singular	el niño simpático *(the nice boy)*	la niña simpática *(the nice girl)*
	plural	los niños simpáticos *(the nice boys)*	las niñas simpáticas *(the nice girls)*

2.1. The inflection of adjectives

● All adjectives agree in gender and number with the noun they qualify. This is why, when you use an adjective, you should pay attention to the gender and number of the noun it modifies.

● All adjectives are inflected to indicate a change in number and many are inflected to indicate a change in gender. In other words, adjectives always have different forms for the singular and plural, and they often have different forms for the masculine and feminine.

2.1.a. Gender

According to the way adjectives vary in relation to gender, they can be classified into two main groups: *adjectives with two endings*, which are inflected according to gender, and *adjectives with one ending*, which are not inflected.

Adjectives with two endings

They have one ending for the masculine and a different ending for the feminine. The feminine always ends in −a. However, the masculine can have different endings.

Masculine: -O	Un paisaje bonito. *(A pretty landscape.)*
Feminine: -A	Una bonita escena. *(A pretty scene.)*
	El negro carbón. *(The black coal.)*
	La negra noche. *(The dark night.)*
	El niño bueno. *(The good boy.)*
	La niña buena. *(The good girl.)*
Masculine: -DOR,	Un alumno trabajador. *(A hard-working student.)*
-TOR, -SER, -ON,	Una alumna trabajadora. *(A hard-working student.)*
-AN, -IN	Un alumno holgazán. *(A lazy student.)*
Feminine: -A	Una alumna holgazana. *(A lazy student.)*
	Un profesor encantador. *(A charming professor.)*
	Una persona encantadora. *(A charming person.)*
Masculine: -OTE,	El perro feote. *(The ugly dog.)*
-ETE	La perra feota. *(The ugly bitch.)*
Feminine: -A	El niño regordete. *(The fat boy.)*
	La niña regordeta. *(The fat girl.)*

Adjectives denoting nationality or regional origin have two endings: the masculine form of the adjective ends in an −o and changes to −a in the feminine, or the masculine form of the adjective ends in a consonant and the feminine is made by adding an −a:

el idioma español *(the Spanish language)*
la lengua española *(the Spanish language)*
el vino francés *(French wine)*
la tortilla francesa *(French omelet)*
el litoral andaluz *(the Andalusian seaside)*
la costa andaluza *(the Andalusian coast)*

Adjectives with one ending

The remaining adjectives are not inflected according to gender. In other words, they have the same form for the masculine and feminine:

una canción triste *(a sad song)*
un final triste *(a sad end)*

un árbol verde *(a green tree)*
una planta verde *(a green plant)*
un chico inteligente *(an intelligent boy)*
una chica inteligente *(an intelligent girl)*

The main adjectives with one ending are as follows:

● Adjectives ending in a consonant that are not included in any of the previous groups: *principal, eficaz, genial,* etc.

● Those ending in −*a* and −*i: homicida, cursi,* etc.

● Most adjectives ending in −*e: increíble, posible, amable,* etc.

2.1.b. Number

All adjectives are inflected to indicate a change in number and have a different form for the singular and plural. The plural is formed by adding −*s* or −*es* to the singular form. In Spanish, the same rules apply to the formation of the plural of adjectives as to the formation of the plural of nouns:

Add −*s* adjectives ending in a non-accented vowel	la hoja verde *(the green leaf)* las hojas verdes *(the green leaves)* una nota breve *(a short note)* unas notas breves *(some short notes)* la rosa roja *(the red rose)* las rosas rojas *(the red roses)*
Add −*s* adjectives ending in an accented vowel	el gobierno israelí *(the Israeli government)* los ciudadanos israelíes *(the Israeli citizens)*
Add −*es* adjectives ending in a consonant	la castaña marrón *(the brown chestnut)* las castañas marrones *(the brown chestnuts)* la abuela feliz *(the happy grandmother)* las abuelas felices *(the happy grandmothers)* la moto azul *(the blue motorcycle)* las motos azules *(the blue motorcycles)*

2.1.c. Agreement

Adjectives always agree in gender and number with the noun they qualify, regardless of their position in the sentence:

2. Adjectives

Tenía unos ojos azules, grandes y muy expresivos.

In English, it should be *She had big, blue and very expressive eyes.*

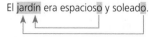

Me he enamorado de sus preciosos ojos azules.

In English, it should be *I've fallen in love with her beautiful blue eyes.*

They also agree with the noun even when they are not placed next to it:

El jardín era espacioso y soleado.

In English, it should be *The garden was spacious and sunny.*

If the adjective qualifies two or more nouns it is always plural, and if one of the nouns is masculine and the other feminine, the gender of the adjective is always masculine:

Luis y Paloma son muy simpáticos. *(Luis and Paloma are very nice.)*
Se puso la blusa y el bolso negros. *(She wore a black blouse and purse.)*

2.2.   The position of adjectives

In Spanish, adjectives may be placed either before or, more frequently, after the noun:

las montañas altas *(the high / tall mountains)*
las altas montañas *(the high / tall mountains)*
unos jardines bonitos *(some pretty gardens)*
unos bonitos jardines *(some pretty gardens)*

Adjectives may also be placed after certain verbs, mainly *ser* and *estar*:

La niña es buena. *(The girl is good.)*
Aquellos perros son muy revoltosos. *(Those dogs are very naughty.)*
La leche está caliente. *(The milk is hot.)*
Su padre está muy delgado. *(Her father is very thin.)*
Gonzalo está feliz. *(Gonzalo is happy.)*

2.2.a. Before or after the noun

Adjectives can be placed before or after the noun. Many adjectives can be placed in either position:

las **frías** aguas *(the* **cold** *waters)*
las aguas **frías** *(the* **cold** *waters)*
tu **dulce** mirada *(the* **tender** *look in your eyes)*
tu mirada **dulce** *(the* **tender** *look in your eyes)*
nuestra **principal** ocupación *(our* **main** *activity)*
nuestra ocupación **principal** *(our* **main** *activity)*

Some adjectives vary in meaning according to their position:

ADJ

un hombre pobre = 'he has no money; he isn't rich'
un pobre hombre = 'he's unfortunate; he's unlucky'

Other adjectives can only be placed after the noun. For example, you have to say *un chico francés (a French boy)*, not **un francés chico*. The main groups of adjectives that fit into this category are:

- Adjectives denoting the place (country, city, etc.) where somebody comes from: *francés (French)*, *inglés (English)*, *americano (American)*, *español (Spanish)*, *madrileño (from Madrid)* etc.

- Many adjectives formed from a noun: *solar (solar)* from *Sol (Sun)*, *constitucional (constitutional)* from *constitución (constitution)*, *territorial (territorial)* from *territorio (territory)*, etc.

2.2.b. Apocopated forms

The form of most adjectives doesn't change when they are placed before or after the noun. However, the singular masculine forms of some adjectives lose their final letters when they are placed before a noun. The shortened form of the adjective is known as the *apocopated* form. Some determiners also have apocopated forms.

The most frequent apocopated forms are:

bueno ⇒ buen	un buen chico *(a good boy)*
	compared with un chico bueno, una buena chica
malo ⇒ mal	un mal amigo *(a bad friend)*
	compared with un amigo malo, una mala amiga
alguno ⇒ algún	algún día llegarán *(they'll arrive some day)*
	compared with alguna semana
ninguno ⇒ ningún	ningún niño *(no boy)*
	compared with ninguna niña

primero ⇒ **primer**	el primer capítulo *(the first chapter)*
	compared with el capítulo primero, la primera parte
tercero ⇒ **tercer**	el tercer capítulo *(the third chapter)*
	compared with el capítulo tercero, la tercera parte
santo ⇒ **san**	san Ignacio *(Saint Ignacio)*
	compared with santa María
grande ⇒ **gran**	un gran palacio *(a large palace)*
	compared with un palacio grande

The adjective *grande* is also apocopated when it precedes a feminine noun: *una gran fiesta (a big party)*, compared with *una casa grande (a large house)*.

2.3. Degrees of comparison

Adjectives denote a property or attribute. In many cases, adjectives have different forms to show the extent or degree to which they show these properties or attributes. These attributes are expressed by *degrees of comparison*.

Adjectives that do not compare the person, thing or place being referred to with anything else are known as positive adjectives. The adjective can also express:

- **Comparative degree:** the property of an adjective is compared with the property of an adjective of another noun.

- **Superlative degree:** indicates the greatest degree of similarity or difference of the adjective that modifies a noun.

2.3.a. The comparative

The comparative indicates the degree of similarity or difference between the nouns being described. There are three types of comparative degrees: superiority, inferiority and equality.

Comparative of superiority

This is formed by placing *más* in front of the adjective and *que* after the adjective:

más + *adjective*: Este edificio es más alto.
(This building is taller.)
más + *adjective* + que: Este edificio es más alto que el otro.
(This building is taller than the other.)

Comparative of inferiority

This is formed by placing *menos* in front of the adjective and *que* after the adjective:

menos + *adjective*: Este capítulo es menos interesante. *(This chapter is less interesting.)*
menos + *adjective* + que: Este capítulo es menos interesante que el anterior.
(This chapter is less interesting than the previous one.)

Comparative of equality

This is formed using the structures *tan... como* and *igual de... que*:

tan + *adjective* + como: Boston es tan bonito como Londres. *(Boston is as pretty as London.)*
igual de + *adjective* (+ que): Carlos es igual de serio que su padre. *(Carlos is as reliable as his father.)*

2.3.b. The superlative

The superlative indicates the greatest degree of similarity or difference between the nouns being described by the adjective. There are two types: the *absolute superlative* and the *relative superlative*.

Absolute superlative

Indicates the highest or lowest degree of similarity or difference between the nouns being described by the adjective. The absolute superlative can be expressed in two ways:

- by placing the adjective *muy* in front of the adjective:

  muy + *adjective*: muy bueno *(very good)*; muy tranquila *(very calm)*

- adding the suffix *−ísimo*, *−ísima*, *−ísimos* or *−ísimas* to the adjective:

  adjective + -ísimo: buenísimo *(the best)*, buenísima *(the best)*, buenísimos *(the best)*, buenísimas *(the best)*

ADJ

Relative superlative

Indicates the highest or lowest degree of similarity or difference expressed by an adjective within the context of a larger group.

The relative superlative is constructed with a definite article (*el, la, los, las*) followed by *más* or *menos* plus the adjective:

> el, la, los, las (+ *noun*) + más + *adjective*: El médico más amable *(The kindest doctor)*; la más bromista *(the most prankster)*
> el, la, los, las (+ *noun*) + menos + *adjective*: El piso menos luminoso *(The darkest room)*; la más rica *(the richest)*

The relative superlative is often followed by an object preceded by the preposition *de* which indicates the word or words the comparison is being made with:

> el médico más amable del hospital *(the kindest doctor in hospital)*
> la más bromista de todas las hermanas *(the most prankster of the sisters)*
> el piso menos luminoso de la escalera *(the darkest apartment on the floor)*
> el más rico de la familia *(the wealthiest of the family)*

2.3.c. Special comparative and superlative forms

The adjectives *bueno, malo, grande* and *pequeño* have special forms to express the comparative and superlative. These are known as the synthetic comparative and superlative:

positive adjective	comparative	
bueno	mejor	Luis es el mejor estudiante de la escuela. *(Luis is the school's best student.)*
malo	peor	Juan es el peor jugador del equipo. *(Juan is the worst player in the team.)*
grande	mayor	Se ha descubierto el mayor caso de corrupción del actual gobierno. *(The biggest corruption case in the present government has been discovered.)*
pequeño	menor	Éste es el menor de los males posibles. *(This is the least possible wrong.)*

positive adjective	superlative	
bueno	óptimo / el mejor	Ha obtenido unos resultados óptimos. *(She has achieved optimum results.)*
malo	pésimo / el peor	Ha hecho un tiempo pésimo. *(We've had very bad weather.)*
grande	máximo / el mayor	Ha obtenido el máximo resultado posible de la prueba. *(He has achieved the best possible results in the test.)*
pequeño	mínimo / el menor	Ocupa el espacio mínimo disponible. *(It occupies the least available room.)*

ADJ

These superlative forms are often used, but the superlative is frequently expressed by the suffix *-ísimo, -ísima, -ísimos* and *-ísimas* or the adverb *muy*:

Obtuvo unos resultados muy buenos. *(She achieved very good results.)*
Obtuvo unos resultados buenísimos. *(She achieved wonderful results.)*
Ha hecho un tiempo muy malo. *(We've had very bad weather.)*
Ha hecho un tiempo malísimo. *(We've had the worst weather.)*

3. Articles

The article always precedes the noun that it defines. In Spanish, the articles are inflected to indicate a change in number and gender. In other words, they have different forms for the masculine and feminine and the singular and plural.

Articles agree in gender and number with the noun they qualify. They allow us to distinguish the gender of nouns as well as to recognize if the word or words they precede are nouns or have the value of a noun.

3.1 Forms

There are two articles in Spanish: the *definite article* and *indefinite article*. They can be recognized by their form and the function they perform.

The forms of the definite and indefinite articles, with their different genders and numbers, are as follows:

	DEFINITE ARTICLE			INDEFINITE ARTICLE	
	masculine	feminine	neutral	masculine	feminine
singular	el	la	lo	un	una
plural	los	las		unos	unas

3.2. Position

In Spanish, the article always goes before the noun:

el pastel de chocolate (*the chocolate cake*)
las carreras de coches (*car races*)
las tazas del desayuno (*the breakfast cups*)
un teléfono nuevo (*a new phone*)
unos peces rojos (*some goldfish*)
lo absurdo de la situación (*the absurdity of the situation*)

Nevertheless, certain words—mainly adjectives—may be placed between the article and the noun to qualify the noun: *los cómodos sillones (the comfortable armchairs)*; *una magnífica vista (a magnificent view)*.

3.3. Agreement

The articles are inflected to indicate a change in number and gender. They must agree in gender and number with the noun they precede:

el niño *(the boy, the child)*   la niña *(the girl, the child)*
los niños *(the boys, the children)*   las niñas *(the girls, the children)*

un gato *(a cat)*   una gata *(a cat)*
unos gatos *(some cats)*   unas gatas *(some cats)*

If a word is placed between the article and the noun, the article also agrees with the word preceding the noun:

un magnífico corredor *(a magnificent runner)*
una magnífica corredora *(a magnificent runner)*
unos magníficos corredores *(some magnificent runners)*
unas magníficas corredoras *(some magnificent runners)*

When the article accompanies two nouns or more that are joined by a conjunction, it agrees in gender and number with the first one:

Avisaron a los niños y niñas de la clase. *(They let the boys and the girls in the class know.)*
Avisaron a las niñas y niños de la clase. *(They let the girls and the boys in the class know.)*

3.4. Function of the article

The definite and indefinite articles provide us with additional information about the noun. The choice of a definite or an indefinite article depends on complex factors which result in a variety of uses. The general rule for choosing between the definite or indefinite article depends on whether the noun it accompanies refers to a person, animal or thing that is known or not known to the listener:

- The definite article is used when the noun has been mentioned previously.

3. Articles

- The indefinite article is used when a noun is mentioned for the first time.

  Ha entrado un hombre. *(A man entered.)* We use the indefinite article because the man is being mentioned for the first time.
  El hombre que ha entrado lleva una camisa gris. *(The man who entered is wearing a gray shirt.)* We use the definite article because the man has been mentioned before.

3.4.a. The definite article

The definite article can be used in several ways.

General rule

The definite article is mainly used to introduce nouns that have been mentioned previously or when the listener knows or can guess from the context the noun referred to:

  Vi un perro y un gato. El perro era negro y el gato era blanco. *(I saw a dog and a cat. The dog was black and the cat was white.)*
  He traído las galletas que me pedisteis. *(I've brought the cookies you asked me for.)*

It is also used to accompany nouns that have not been mentioned previously but which refer to realities already identified in the minds of those who are speaking.

This occurs in the following cases:

- When the existence of the noun being referred to can be deduced due to our knowledge of the world:

  Subimos a un autobús. El conductor era muy simpático. *(We got on a bus. The driver was very nice.)*
  Quiero hablar con el director de la oficina. *(I want to speak to the office manager.)*

- When there is only one in existence:

  El Papa *(The Pope)*
  El presidente de los Estados Unidos *(The president of the United States)*
  La Luna *(The Moon)*

- The noun refers to a reality that we are aware of:

  Busco las gafas que perdí la semana pasada. *(I'm looking for the glasses that I lost last week.)*
  Éste es el chico del que te hablé el otro día. *(This is the boy I was telling you about the other day.)*

Other uses

The definite article has other uses than the ones described. The main ones are listed below:

a) Before nouns used in a general sense:

El perro es un mamífero. *(Dogs are mammals.)*
La verdura es necesaria para una alimentación equilibrada. *(Vegetables are necessary for a balanced diet.)*
La energía solar es una energía limpia. *(Solar energy is a clean energy.)*

b) Before numbers indicating the time of the day:

Es la una. *(It's one o'clock.)*
Son las doce y cuarto de la noche. *(It's a quarter after midnight.)*

c) Before the days of the week:

El domingo fuimos en bicicleta. *(We went for a bike ride on Sunday.)*

d) Before some proper nouns:

● With the names of people when preceded by their title and when their surname is specified:

la señora Arias *(Mrs. Arias)*
el doctor Turner *(Doctor Turner)*
el presidente Juan Blasco *(President Juan Blasco)*

● With the names of public places, such as hotels, theaters, museums and hospitals:

el museo Reina Sofía *(the Reina Sofia Museum)*
el Hospital General *(the General Hospital)*
la Universidad Complutense *(Complutense University)*

● With geographical names, such as rivers, seas and mountains:

el (mar) Mediterráneo *(the Mediterranean [Sea])*
las islas Canarias *(the Canary Islands)*
las Rocosas *(the Rockies)*

● With the names of streets, squares, avenues, etc.:

la calle Valencia *(Valencia Street)*
la Quinta Avenida *(Fifth Avenue)*
la plaza de la Independencia *(Independence Square)*

3.4.b. The indefinite article

The indefinite article can be used in a wide variety of ways.

General rule

The indefinite article is mainly used to introduce nouns when the listener does not know or cannot guess from the context the noun being referred to:

Se ha comprado una casa en las afueras. *(He's bought a house on the outskirts.)*
Tienen unos muebles preciosos. *(They have some beautiful furniture.)*

For the same reason, the indefinite article is used with the verb *haber*:

Hay una gran casa en la esquina. *(There's a large house on the corner.)*
En el salón había un gran sillón. *(There was a big armchair in the living room.)*

Other uses

The indefinite article has other uses. The main ones are listed below:

- It refers to something non-specific:

    Préstame un lápiz. *(Lend me a pencil.)*
    La niña necesita una carpeta. *(The girl needs a folder.)*
    Me han regalado unas flores. *(They've given me some flowers.)*

- It identifies something that is part of a group.

    Es un gato siamés. *(It's a Siamese cat.)*
    Esto es una estafa. *(This is a rip-off.)*
    Es un jersey de pura lana virgen. *(It's a pure virgin wool sweater.)*

- It indicates degrees of intensity:

    Tengo un hambre que me muero. *(I'm starving.)*
    Hace un frío terrible. *(It's bitterly cold.)*

3.4.c. The neutral form

Lo is the neutral form of the definite article. It has no plural. *Lo* cannot be used before a noun because there are no neuter nouns in Spanish.

The basic function of the neutral article *lo* is to change the word it accompanies into a noun. It is mainly used in the following cases:

● With adjectives:

Me sorprende lo claro que está, a pesar de lo difícil que parecía. *(I'm surprised how clear it is, in spite of how difficult it seemed.)*

● With subordinate clauses:

Lo que contaste el otro día me gustó. *(I liked what you told me the other day.)*
Lo que querría saber es por qué lo has hecho. *(What I wanted to know is why you did it.)*

It can also appear with adverbs in exclamative clauses:

¡Lo bien que lo hace! *(He does it really well!)*

3.5. Use and omission of the article

As a general rule, nouns are always accompanied by an article in Spanish. The use or omission of an article depends on the syntactical function of the noun.

The article must be used when the noun is the subject of the sentence:

El pescado es muy saludable. *(Fish is very healthy.)*
Un hombre entró por la puerta. *(A man came in through the door.)*

The article can only be omitted when the noun is the subject of the sentence and the subject follows the verb. There are few such verbs: *llegar, salir, entrar, nacer* or *morir.* This is only possible:

● If the noun is uncountable:

Entra gente constantemente. *(People keep coming in.)*

● If the noun is plural:

Llegan trenes cada hora. *(Trains run every hour.)*

When the noun is not the subject of the sentence, the article can be omitted in the following cases:

● If the noun is uncountable:

Bebe leche cada día. *(He drinks milk every day.)*

● When the noun does not refer to a specific object, but to a class of objects, particularly if it is placed after a preposition:

Ha llegado en autocar. *(He came by bus.)*

3.6. Special rules

3.6.a. The article before feminine nouns beginning with *a*

The definite article *el* is used with masculine nouns in the singular because the article must agree in gender and number with the noun it refers to. However, *el* is also used when it precedes a singular feminine noun beginning with a stressed *a* or *ha*:

el agua *(water)*
el águila *(the eagle)*
el hacha *(the ax)*

In these cases, the masculine article is only used when:

- the noun is singular: el *agua (water)*, but las *aguas (the waters)*.

- there are no other words placed between the article and the noun: *el agua (the water)*, but *la fría agua del río (the cold water of the river)*.

The same rule applies to the indefinite article *un*, but in this case this usage is not compulsory but optional. In other words, when an indefinite article precedes a feminine noun beginning with a stressed *a* or *ha*:

- The masculine form can be used:

un agua *(a water)*
un águila *(an eagle)*
un hacha *(an ax)*

- Or the feminine form can be used:

una agua *(a water)*
una águila *(an eagle)*
una hacha *(an ax)*

3.6.b. Contractions *a + el* and *de + el*

The prepositions *a* and *de* contract with the masculine singular definite article *el* to form *al* and *del*. They do not contract with the feminine *la* or the plurals *los* and *las*:

- **a + el = al** Vamos al parque cada mañana. *(We go to the park every morning.)*
- **de + el = del** El precio del gas ha subido mucho este año. *(The price of gas has gone up a lot this year.)*

4. Pronouns and determiners

In Spanish, pronouns and determiners make up a class of words that can be divided into several subclasses. Each of these subclasses performs a different function and is used in a different way. The members of some of these subclasses can only be used as pronouns. In other words, they can occupy the position of the noun they replace but cannot accompany a noun. This is the case, for instance, with the personal pronouns *yo, tú* and *él*. However, the members of other subclasses can also act as determiners; in other words, they can precede the noun and perform the same function as the article. Some pronouns and determiners can also perform other syntactical functions, such as an adjective or noun.

The subclasses of pronouns in Spanish are as follows:

- Personal: *yo (I), tú (you), él (he)*, etc.

- Possessive: *mío (mine), tuyo (yours), suyo (his)*, etc.

- Demonstrative: *este (this), ese (that), aquel (that)*, etc.

- Indefinite: *alguno (some), ninguno (neither / none), bastante (enough)*, etc.

- Numeral: *uno (one), dos (two), tres (three)*, etc.

- Interrogative: *qué (what?), cuál (which?), quién (who?)*, etc.

- Relative: *que (that / which), quien (who), el cual (who)*, etc.

4.1. Personal pronouns

Personal pronouns are used to refer to the specific participants in a discourse: the speaker, the addressee (the person or people being spoken to) or a third party (the person or people being spoken about). These participants are known as persons.

1st person	the speaker or a group including the speaker
2nd person	the addressee or a group including the addressee
3rd person	somebody or something different from the speaker or the addressee

Personal pronouns have different forms for masculine, feminine, singular and plural. The forms also vary according to the syntactical function they perform:

- Subject forms

- Direct and indirect object forms without a preposition

- Object forms following a preposition

- Reflexive forms

All personal pronouns have different forms for the singular and plural, and some are inflected to indicate a change in gender.

4.1.a. Subject pronouns

In Spanish, the subject pronouns are always stressed. Each grammatical person takes a different form in the singular and plural.

These pronouns refer to people. With the exception of the pronoun *ello*, they cannot refer to inanimate objects. The form *ello*, can only be used to refer to inanimate objects but never to people.

Forms

There are dialectical variants of the subject pronouns in Spanish. In other words, there are differences in the forms of the subject pronoun used in Spain and other Spanish-speaking countries. There is a standard system in Spain which is the most widely used, and other standard systems that are used in different regions of Latin America. These differences mainly concern the second-person singular (*tú*, in Spain, compared with *vos* in Argentina, for example, or the use of *usted* in the second-person singular) and the plural (*vosotros*, in Spain, compared with the use of *ustedes* for the second-person plural in Latin America).

Standard system

The standard system is used throughout Spain, with the exception of the Canary Islands and some parts of Andalusia. It is sometimes used in formal language and written texts in other Spanish-speaking countries.

The subject pronouns corresponding to the three grammatical persons in the standard system are as follows:

Person	Singular	Plural
1st person	yo *(I)*	nosotros, nosotras *(we)*
2nd person	tú *(you)*	vosotros, vosotras *(you)*
(polite form)	usted *(you)*	ustedes *(you)*
3rd person	él, ella, ello *(he, she, it)*	ellos, ellas *(they)*

The first and second-person plural, and the third-person plural forms agree in gender; in other words, their ending varies according to the gender of the noun being referred to.

The forms usted *and* ustedes

The pronouns *usted* and *ustedes* are used as polite forms to refer to the second person in the discourse (the addressee or interlocutor). However, from a grammatical viewpoint, they are third-person pronouns and, as such, must agree with the third person of the verb:

Usted no conoce bien la ciudad. *(You don't know the city well.)*
Ustedes, ¿qué quieren saber exactamente? *(What exactly do you want to know?)*

In the standard system, the difference between *tú / vosotros* and *usted / ustedes* depends on the degree of familiarity or respect you wish to convey: *tú / vosotros* is used in informal situations, when you know or are close to the person you are speaking to, when you are talking to someone of the same age and rank, or when you do not consider it necessary to address somebody formally. *Usted* and *ustedes* are used in situations when you need to show respect for the person you are speaking to: when speaking to someone in a position of authority, with someone older or someone you do not know well. As a general rule, when you are speaking to a person with a title such as *Señor, Señora, Doctor, Profesor*, you should use *usted* and *ustedes*. In present-day Spanish, we tend to avoid using *usted* and *ustedes* to speak to young people.

In some regions of Spain and Spanish-speaking countries, the use of *usted* and *ustedes* is not exactly the same as in standard Spanish. Nevertheless, in all cases, these pronouns refer to the second-person singular or plural (the addressee or interlocutor) and, from a grammatical viewpoint, they are third-person pronouns and, therefore, must agree with the third person of the verb.

Subject pronouns in Latin American Spanish

The dialectical differences between the subject pronouns in European and Latin American Spanish only occur in the second-person forms. In all cases, the singular distinguishes between a familiar form (*tú* or *vos*), and a polite form (*usted*). In the plural, there is only one form (*ustedes*) which is used regardless of the speaker's level of familiarity with the addressee or interlocutor.

In Latin American Spanish there are three different systems:

- The first system is used in some parts of Spain—parts of Andalusia and the Canary Islands—and in some Latin American countries: Mexico, Peru and parts of Colombia and Venezuela. It uses the following forms:

	Singular	Plural
Familiarity	tú	ustedes
Politeness	usted	

- The second system is more widespread in Latin American Spanish. It is used in Chile, Ecuador, many areas of Colombia and Venezuela, in parts of Panama and Costa Rica, and in Uruguay. It uses the following forms:

	Singular	Plural
Familiarity	vos / tú	ustedes
Politeness	usted	

- The third system is used in Argentina, Nicaragua, Guatemala, Paraguay and parts of El Salvador, Honduras and Costa Rica. It uses the following forms:

	Singular	Plural
Familiarity	vos	ustedes
Politeness	usted	

The use of *vos* in the second and third system is a phenomenon known as *voseo*. *Voseo* is the use of the second-person singular pronoun *vos* instead of *tú*.

Use of subject pronouns

Spanish is a "null-subject" language. This means that, unlike English, subject pronouns are not usually expressed and are often omitted because the verb endings vary, making the pronouns unnecessary.

In Spanish, personal pronouns are generally omitted:

> Voy a comprar las sillas. *(I'm going to buy the chairs.)*
> ¿Cómo te llamas? *(What is your name?)*
> Espera que lo llames. *(He expects you to call.)*
> Creo que iremos al cine el martes. *(I think we'll go to the movies on Tuesday.)*
> ¿Cuándo empezáis las vacaciones? *(When will you start your vacation?)*
> Tocan cada noche en el mismo bar. *(They play every night at the same bar.)*

PRON & DET

Subject pronouns are only used for emphasis or to avoid ambiguity. Basically, subject pronouns are used in the three following cases:

● To emphasize the subject and contrast what is being said or has been said about the subject, or what is implied about other subjects:

> Yo sí quiero hacer las paces. *(I do want to make up.)* It implies that other people do not want to settle their differences.
> Tú jamás cambiarás de opinión. *(You will never change your mind.)* It implies that other people do want to change their minds.

● To show a contrast between two subjects:

> Yo busco unos pantalones y tú buscas una blusa. *(I am looking for some pants and you are seaching for a blouse.)*
> Juan no ha de ir a buscar a los niños, has de ir tú. *(Juan is not going to pick up the children, you are.)*

● To avoid ambiguity. For example, when two people or things have been mentioned in a previous sentence or statement and the omission of the subject pronoun would lead to confusion about which of them is being referred to:

> Juan conoció a María en un bar. Ella estaba tomando un café.
> *(Juan met María in a bar. She was having coffee.)*

4.1.b. Direct and indirect object pronouns without a preposition

Nouns that are the direct and indirect objects of a sentence can be replaced by direct and indirect object pronouns. In this case, the preposition *a* disappears. These pronouns are known as *pronombres átonos* or unstressed pronouns and they are always placed next to the verbs they complement.

The forms of the first and second-person direct and indirect object pronouns are only used to refer to people or animate beings. The third-person forms can refer to people as well as inanimate objects.

Forms

The direct and indirect object pronouns are as follows:

PERSON	SINGULAR		PLURAL	
	Direct object	Indirect object	Direct object	Indirect object
1st person	me	me	nos	nos
2nd person	te	te	os	os
(polite form)	lo, la	le / se	los, las	les / se
3rd person	lo, la	le / se	los, las	les / se

The second-person object pronouns have the familiar forms *te* and *os* (the equivalent of the subject pronouns *tú* and *vosotros*) and the polite forms *lo, la, los, las* and *le, les* (the equivalent of the subject pronouns *usted* and *ustedes*).

Leísmo, laísmo *and* loísmo

In some Spanish-speaking countries, particularly in Spain, the third-person object pronouns are often used interchangeably. This usage is known as *leísmo, laísmo* and *loísmo*.

● *Leísmo* is a widespread phenomenon in Spain. It involves using the form *le* for the indirect and direct object:

Vi a Juan. *(I saw Juan.)*
Standard form: lo vi
Leísmo form: le vi

Leísmo is very frequent when the direct object pronoun refers to a person, particularly in the singular, but it is seldom used in the plural and is very infrequent when the direct object pronoun refers to inanimate beings or objects.

● *Laísmo* and *loísmo* are much less frequent phenomena and are only used in some parts of Spain. They involve the use of the forms *la* and *lo* for the feminine and masculine indirect object pronouns.

Use of direct and indirect object pronouns without a preposition

Unstressed personal pronouns always perform the function of direct or indirect objects.

When the full noun form of the direct object appears in a sentence, the direct object pronoun *lo* cannot be used in the same sentence:

> Vi a Juan. *(I saw Juan.)*
> Lo vi. *(I saw him.)*
> But not *lo vi a Juan.

However, the indirect object pronoun is often used, even when the full noun form of the indirect object appears in the sentence:

> Le di el libro. *(I gave him the book.)*
> Le di el libro a Juan. *(I gave Juan the book.)*

Position

Unstressed personal pronouns are always attached to the verb, meaning that no words can be placed between the pronoun and the verb. These pronouns can be placed before the verb as a separate word (*lo dijo*), or attached to the verb to form a single word (*decirlo*). In standard Spanish, pronouns go before all the forms of the verb, except for the imperative, infinitive and gerund:

● They always go before the conjugated forms of the verb (except in the imperative): *lo haces, lo haré, lo haría, lo haremos…*

● They always go after the verb with the imperative, infinitive and gerund: *hazlo, hacerlo, haciéndolo.*

In early forms of Spanish, the pronoun was appended to other verbal forms. Nowadays, it looks old-fashioned if we add the pronoun to forms other than the infinitive. This practice only survives in some Latin American Spanish dialects.

The personal pronoun can be placed before a conjugated form of the verb that is followed by an infinitive or gerund:

> Quiero hacerlo. *(I want to do it.)*
> Lo quiero hacer. *(I want to do it.)*
> Intentó hacerlo. *(He tried to do it.)*
> Lo intentó hacer. *(He tried to do it.)*

In these cases, when a verb takes two object pronouns, both of them must appear in the same order:

> Quiero dárselo. *(I want to give it to her.)*
> Se lo quiero dar. *(I want to give it to her.)*

Combination

When a direct and an indirect object pronoun occur with the same verb, they appear in the sentence as follows:

- The second-person pronouns precede the first-person direct object pronouns: *te me ofreciste (you volunteered to me)*; *te nos ofreciste (you volunteered to us)*.

- The first- and second-person pronouns precede the third-person pronouns: *me lo regalaron (they gave it to me)*; *te lo regalaron (they gave it to you)*.

- The pronoun *se* always comes first: *se me cayó (I dropped it)*; *se te cayó (you dropped it)*; *se le cayó (he dropped it)*.

When the third-person pronouns *le* and *les* are combined with the pronouns *lo, la, los, las* they change to *se*:

> Le dije esto. *(I told him this.)* Se lo dije.
> Les dije esto. *(I told them this.)* Se lo dije.

4.1.c. Reflexive pronouns

Reflexive pronouns are used to refer back to the object of the verb when the subject of a verb is also its object.

(Yo) Me he comprado un abrigo. *(I bought myself a coat.)*

Mi vecina se puso el delantal antes de cocinar. *(My neighbor put on her apron before cooking.)*

El niño se lavó la cara. *(The boy washed his face.)*

Forms

The reflexive pronouns are as follows:

Person	Singular	Plural
1st person	me	nos
2nd person	te	os
(polite form)	se	se
3rd person	se	se

The polite forms of the second-person pronoun are used when the subject is *usted*.

Use of reflexive pronouns

Reflexive pronouns are generally used when the subject pronoun and object pronoun refer to the same person or thing. They also express a reciprocal action; in other words, when the subject is plural, they can have the same meaning as *el uno al otro* (each other, one another):

No nos vemos desde hace tiempo (el uno al otro). *(We haven't seen each other in a long time.)*

Se saludaron (el uno al otro) con gran afecto. *(They greeted each other very fondly.)*

4.1.d. Object pronouns following a preposition

In Spanish, there are specific forms for personal pronouns when they are placed after a preposition. These pronouns can be used after any preposition, including the preposition *a*, which introduces the indirect and direct object pronoun:

PRON
& DET

4. Pronouns and determiners

con él *(with him)*   sin mí *(without me)*
a ti *(to you)*   sobre nosotros *(about us)*

These pronouns are always stressed. Some of them have the same form as the subject pronouns, but others are different. Just like the subject pronouns, these pronouns only refer to people and cannot refer to inanimate objects (with the exception of the pronoun *ello*).

Forms

The forms of the stressed personal pronouns placed after a preposition are as follows:

Person	Singular		Plural
1st person	mí	(conmigo)	nosotros, nosotras
2nd person	ti	(contigo)	vosotros, vosotras
(polite form)	usted / sí	(consigo)	ustedes / sí
3rd person	él, ella, ello / sí	(consigo)	ellos, ellas / sí

There are familiar forms and polite forms for the second-person singular and plural which are distributed in the same way as their equivalent subject pronoun forms.

Third-person pronouns, as well as the second-person polite forms (*usted* and *ustedes*), have a special form when they are reflexive; in other words, when the object is the same as the subject. In these cases, the form *sí* can be used, in both singular and plural:

Juan habla de sí mismo. *(Juan speaks about himself.)*

However, the *sí* form is formal or literary in style. In spoken Spanish, the other forms of the stressed pronouns are used instead of *sí*: *Juan habla de él mismo. (Juan speaks about himself.)*

Use of object pronouns following a preposition

The stressed personal pronouns can be placed after any preposition, with the exception of the examples given below, and perform any function, except for the subject of the sentence:

Este regalo es para ti. *(This present is for you.)*
Estoy segura de que hablabas de mí. *(I'm sure you were talking about me.)*
Delante de él, todos callaban. *(They all kept silence in front of him.)*
Lo hizo por nosotras. *(He did it for us.)*
Se lo dio a él. *(She gave it to him.)*

Special cases

There are two other important exceptions in the singular when stressed personal pronouns cannot be used after a preposition:

- In the first and second person, the subject pronouns *yo* and *tú* must be used after the prepositions *entre*, *hasta* and *según*:

  Lo dirigiréis entre tú y él. *(You'll manage it between you two.)*
  Hasta yo me he enfadado. *(Even I am angry.)*
  Según tú, todo es muy fácil. *(According to you, it's all very easy.)*

- After the preposition *con*, they must be replaced by the forms *conmigo*, *contigo* and *consigo*:

  Ven conmigo. *(Come with me.)*
  Me gusta hablar contigo. *(I like talking with you.)*
  Siempre habla consigo. *(He always talks to himself.)*

4.2. Possessives

Possessives express the possession of an item by an individual. For example:

  mi coche *(my car)*
  tu lápiz *(your pencil)*
  este libro es mío *(this book is mine)*

They can also indicate a special relationship between an object and a person:

  tu hijo *(your son)*
  mis vacaciones *(my vacation)*
  su libro *(his book)* (= 'the book he wrote')

The possessive can often be replaced by a prepositional phrase formed by the preposition *de* and the name of the possessor:

  su hijo *(her son)*
  el hijo de Marta *(Marta's son)*

4.2.a. Forms

There are different possessive forms for the three grammatical persons, both singular and plural. Their usage depends on who the possessor is: the speaker, the addressee or a third party. The possessives are also inflected to indicate a change in number and are sometimes inflected to indicate a change in gender.

There are two different series: full forms and apocopated forms.

Full forms

The full forms are stressed words that are inflected to indicate a change in gender and number.

Person	Singular	Plural
1st person	mío, mía, míos, mías	nuestro, nuestra, nuestros, nuestras
2nd person	tuyo, tuya, tuyos, tuyas	vuestro, vuestra, vuestros, vuestras
3rd person	suyo, suya, suyos, suyas	suyo, suya, suyos, suyas

The third-person forms are the same in the singular and plural.

Apocopated forms

The apocopated forms are unstressed words. They are inflected to indicate a change in number, but not gender.

There are apocopated forms for the first- and second-person singular and the third-person singular and plural. The full forms are used for the first- and second-person plural.

Person	Singular	Plural
1st person	mi, mis	*the full form is used:* nuestro, nuestra, nuestros, nuestras
2nd person	tu, tus	*the full form is used:* vuestro, vuestra, vuestros, vuestras
3rd person	su, sus	su, sus

The third-person forms are the same for the singular and plural.

4.2.b. Function of possessives

The full-form and apocopated possessives perform different functions and, as a result, are placed in different positions.

Full forms

The full forms of the possessives are used:

● As pronouns; in other words, they replace a noun. In these cases, they can appear with or without a determiner:

Me gusta más esta casa que la mía. *(I like this house better than mine.)*
Estos lápices son míos. *(These pencils are mine.)*

● As adjectives, following the noun. The noun retains the article:

Estas ideas suyas siempre nos traen problemas. *(These ideas of his always bring us trouble.)*
Me encontré a un primo tuyo en un bar. *(I found a cousin of yours in a bar.)*

Apocopated forms

The apocopated forms of the possessives are used as determiners. In other words, they precede the noun:

mi padre *(my father)*
mi ordenador portátil *(my portable PC)*
mi moto *(my motorcycle)*
¿Me puedes dar tu dirección de correo electrónico? *(Can you give me your e-mail address?)*

The apocopated forms cannot be accompanied by the article because they act as determiners:

mi hermano *(my brother)*, but not *el mi hermano or *un mi hermano

The full forms of the first- and second-person plural are also used as determiners, as they do not have apocopated forms:

nuestro coche *(our car)*
nuestro ordenador *(our PC)*
vuestra moto *(your motorcycle)*

PRON
& DET

4.2.c. Agreement

In order to decide which form of the possessive to use, you need to take into account who the possessor is and choose the first, second or third person —as well as the forms of the singular or plural— accordingly. For example:

mi casa *(my house)* ⇒ *possessor =* yo
tu casa *(your house)* ⇒ *possessor =* tú
nuestra casa *(our house)* ⇒ *possessor =* nosotros

However, the possessive pronoun does not agree in gender or number with the possessor, but agrees with the item that is possessed. The full forms agree in gender and number, whereas the apocopated forms only agree in number:

mi (Ø) gato (Ø) *(my cat)*

mis gatos *(my cats)*

un gato mío *(my cat)*

una gata mía *(my cat)*

unas gatas mías *(some of my cats)*

4.3.   Demonstratives

Demonstratives indicate the closeness or distance of an object in relation to the speaker or addressee. The closeness or distance of the object can be in space or time:

distance in space: Quiero aquel pastel, por favor. *(I want that cake, please.)*
distance in time: ¿Te acuerdas de aquel día? *(Do your remember that day?)*

Due to their function, demonstratives are closely related to adverbs of place: *aquí* and *acá, ahí, allí* and *allá.*

4.3.a. Forms

There are three demonstrative determiners and pronouns in Spanish. Each one varies in gender and number:

	SINGULAR		PLURAL	
masculine	feminine	neutral	masculine	feminine
este	esta	esto	estos	estas
ese	esa	eso	esos	esas
aquel	aquella	aquello	aquellos	aquellas

4.3.b. Function of demonstratives

Function and position

Demonstratives can perform three different syntactical functions:

- They can appear immediately before the noun:

  este árbol *(this tree)*
  aquel año *(that year)*
  esos hombres *(those men)*

In these cases, they are determiners and cannot be accompanied by the article: *ese hombre (that man)*, but not **el ese hombre.*

- They can appear after the noun. In these cases, they are also adjectives. This means that the noun they accompany can be preceded by an article:

  el verano aquel *(that summer)*
  el profesor ese del que te hablé *(that profesor I talked to you about)*

When demonstratives are placed after a noun, they often have a derogatory meaning.

- Demonstratives have a pronominal use when they replace a noun:

  Deme ese, por favor. *(Give that one, please.)*
  Este es el profesor del que te hablé. *(This is the professor I spoke to you about.)*

When they are pronouns, the demonstratives are usually written with an accent (with the exception of the neutral forms *esto, eso, aquello*).

The neutral forms of the demonstrative (*esto, eso, aquello*) are always pronouns. In other words, they can never be accompanied by a noun. The neutral forms are never written with an accent.

4. Pronouns and determiners

Value and use

Demonstratives can be interpreted according to the context of a conversation, or the discourse or text they are part of.

Context based interpretation.	Quiero esto. *(I want this.)*
Discourse based interpretation.	Han venido Juan y María. Esta estaba enfadada. *(Juan and María came. She was angry.)*

In grammatical terminology, context-based demonstratives are said to have a **diectic value** (diectic meaning that they are dependent on the context in which they are used); and discourse-based demonstratives are said to have an **anaphoric value** (the demonstrative replaces a word used earlier). The choice between the three possible forms of the demonstrative depends on whether they are context-based or discourse-based. In other words, their use differs according to their relationship to the thing they are interpreting.

Diectic value

When the demonstratives are diectic, they can express physical distance or closeness, or distance or closeness in time. In the first case, the demonstratives refer to the persons of the discourse: the choice of one form or another depends on the closeness of the speaker or addressee:

este, esta, esto	*Indicates closeness to the speaker.*
estos, estas	Este libro ⇒ *indicates a book that is close to the speaker.*
ese, esa, eso	*Indicates closeness to the addressee.*
esos, esas	Ese libro ⇒ *indicates a book that is close to the addressee.*
aquel, aquella, aquello	*Indicates distance from the speaker and addressee.*
aquellos, aquellas	Aquel libro ⇒ *indicates a book that is far from the speaker and the addressee.*

The demonstrative forms *este*, *ese* and *aquel* are used to express distance in time:

- *Este* and its inflected forms are used for units of time that continue in the present, that have some relation to the present or happened recently:

  Este año iré de vacaciones a Argentina. *(This year I'll go to Argentina on vacation.)*
  Esta mañana me he encontrado a Miguel. *(I saw Miguel this morning.)*

- *Ese, aquel* and their inflected forms are used for units of time that have little or no relation to the present or happened some time ago. In general, *aquel* is used to refer to something farther away than *ese*:

En aquella época aún no lo conocíamos. *(We didn't know him at that time.)*
Quería empezar mis estudios en 2008, pero ese año tuve mucho trabajo.
(I wanted to start studying in 2008, but I had lots of work that year.)

Anaphoric value

When demonstratives are anaphoric, they refer to elements already mentioned in the discourse or text. In these cases, the choice of the demonstrative form depends on several factors:

- The combination of *este / aquel* with their inflected forms is used to refer to two elements. *Aquel* refers to somebody or something farther away in the discourse or text and *este* refers to somebody or something closer:

Entraron Guillermo y Francisco. Este estaba enfadado y aquel estaba contento.

In English, *Guillermo and Francisco came in. The latter was angry and the former was happy.*

- The neutral form *esto* is used to refer to an element in the speaker's own discourse or text:

Lo hemos hecho sin preguntárselo, y esto es un error. *(We didn't ask him before doing it, and that is a mistake.)*

- The neutral form *eso* is mainly used to refer to the previous discourse or text as a whole:

Lo hemos hecho sin preguntárselo. Además, no nos hemos informado y nos estamos precipitando. Eso *(everything that was said previously)* es un error. *(We didn't ask him before doing it. Besides, we are not informed and we are hastening. That is a mistake.)*

- We also use *eso* to refer to an element in someone else's discourse or text:

Person A: —Lo hemos hecho sin preguntárselo. *(We didn't ask him before doing it.)*
Person B: —Sí. Y eso es un error. *(Yes. And that is a mistake.)*

- Finally, *ese* and its inflected forms are used to refer to elements that have appeared previously in the discourse or text:

PRON & DET

> París tiene una catedral. Esa catedral es muy famosa. *(Paris has a cathedral. That cathedral is very famous.)*

4.3.c. Agreement

Demonstrative determiners always agree with the noun they accompany and demonstrative pronouns always agree with the noun they replace:

> A este niño lo conozco, pero a aquel no. *(I know this boy, but not that one.)*
> A esta niña la conozco, pero a aquella no. *(I know this girl, but not that one.)*
> A estos niños los conozco, pero a aquellos no. *(I know these boys, buy not those.)*

The neutral forms can only be used to refer to objects but never to refer to people. They never agree with the noun they refer to. In other words, they can be used to refer to any situation, regardless of whether the noun that designates the situation is masculine, feminine, singular or plural:

> Esto es un lápiz. *(This is a pencil.)*
> Eso es una carpeta. *(That is a folder.)*
> Eso son golondrinas y aquello son palomas. *(These are swallows and those are doves.)*

4.4. Indefinite adjectives and pronouns

Indefinite determiners and pronouns are used to express an indefinite idea of quality or quantity:

> Hay muchos estudiantes en el aula. *(There are many students in the classroom.)*
> Llegaron bastantes turistas. *(Enough tourists have arrived.)*

Some of them only refer to objects, others refer only to people, and some refer to objects and people.

4.4.a. Forms

Indefinites are classified into two groups:

- The first group comprises a series of words that can only act as pronouns. These pronouns are not inflected (with the exception of *quienquiera*, which is inflected to indicate a change in number):

nadie *(nobody, no one)*
alguien *(somebody, someone)*

quienquiera (and quienesquiera) *(whoever)*
nada *(nothing)*
algo *(something)*

- The second group comprises a series of words that are inflected to indicate a change in number. Some of them are inflected to indicate a change in gender. They can be pronouns or adjectives:

SINGULAR		PLURAL	
masculine	feminine	masculine	feminine
algún, alguno	alguna	algunos	algunas
ningún, ninguno	ninguna	—	—
mucho	mucha	muchos	muchas
poco	poca	pocos	pocas
bastante		bastantes	
—	—	varios	varias
demasiado	demasiada	demasiados	demasiadas
cualquier, cualquiera		cualesquiera	
todo	toda	todos	todas
otro	otra	otros	otras

4.4.b. Function of indefinite adjectives and pronouns

General uses

Indefinite determiners and pronouns are used to indicate approximate quantity, degree or intensity.

First group

The indefinites in the first group refer to something or someone indefinite. They can only be used as pronouns. In other words, they can never accompany a noun but must stand alone:

Nadie lo sabe. *(Nobody knows.)*
Hay algo aquí dentro. *(There's something in here.)*

4. Pronouns and determiners

These pronouns are not inflected and, as a result, they do not agree with the noun they replace.

Second group

The indefinites in the second group, like the members of the first, can stand alone as pronouns:

Tenemos demasiados. *(We have too many.)*
¿Me das otra? *(May I have another one?)*

Unlike the pronouns in the first group, these pronouns are inflected and, as a result, must agree with the noun they replace:

Aquí hay una silla y allí hay otra. *(Here we have a chair and there is another.)*

Aquí hay un sillón y allí hay otro. *(Here we have an armchair and there is another.)*

When they accompany a noun, these indefinites perform the function of determiners. In these cases, they usually precede the noun, although they are sometimes placed after the noun.

- In the plural, they are used with countable nouns to indicate an indeterminate number:

  Tengo bastantes ideas para el fin de semana. *(I have enough ideas for the weekend.)*
  Hay pocas personas que lo puedan hacer. *(There are few people who can do it.)*

- In the singular, they are often used with uncountable nouns to indicate an indeterminate quantity:

  Este pastel lleva bastante mantequilla. *(This cake takes plenty of butter.)*
  Queda poco tiempo para acabar. *(We'll finish shortly.)*

Uses as adverbs

The indefinites *algo*, *nada*, *mucho*, *poco*, *bastante* and *demasiado* can also perform the function of adverbs:

—¿Has dormido algo esta noche? *(Have you slept something tonight?)*
—No. No he podido dormir nada. *(No. I have slept nothing.)*

When they are adverbs, they are always used in the masculine singular form.

Particular rules

Negative forms

The indefinites *nadie*, *nada* and *ninguno* have a negative meaning. However, from a syntactical viewpoint, they show certain peculiarities when forming negative sentences:

- When they follow the verb, the verb must be negated:

  No lo sabe nadie. *(Nobody knows.)*

- However, when they precede the verb, no other negation is required:

  Nadie lo sabe. *(Nobody knows.)*

Forms that are only singular or only plural

The indefinite determiner and pronoun *varios* can only be used in the plural:

He ido a varios conciertos de este cantante. *(I've been in many of this singer's concerts.)*
Me gustaría tener varios. *(I would like to have many.)*

Ninguno is never used in the plural:

No hay ninguna chica que me guste. *(There's not one girl that I like.)*

However, you cannot say *no hay ningunas chicas que me gusten. When the noun is plural, the determiner is omitted: *no hay chicas que me gusten.*

Special singular forms

Alguno and *ninguno* drop the last letter when they precede a masculine singular noun:

Algún profesor te lo podrá explicar. *(Some teacher could explain it to you.)*.
But:
Alguna profesora te lo podrá explicar. *(Some teacher could explain it to you.)*
Alguno te lo podrá explicar. *(Someone could explain it to you.)*

Likewise, *cualquiera* drops its last letter when it precedes a masculine or feminine singular noun:

Cualquier persona lo sabe. *(Any person knows.)*.
But: Cualquiera lo sabe. *(Anyone knows.)*

PRON
& DET

4. Pronouns and determiners

Uses with the article

As a general rule of thumb, indefinites are not used with the article or any other determiner. However, there are some exceptions:

a) When *todo* precedes a noun, it can take an article or another determiner. The article or determiner are compulsory when the noun is plural:

Todos los chicos lo sabían. *(All the boys knew.)*
Todos estos chicos lo sabían. *(All these boys knew.)*

In the singular, the meaning of the sentence changes if the article is used or omitted:

- If the article is used, it refers to something in its entirety:

  Se ha manchado toda la camisa. *(He has stained all his shirt.)*

- If the article is omitted, it expresses a general meaning. The meaning is very similar to the use of the plural form:

  Todo hombre es mortal. *(All men are mortal.)*

b) *Poco*, *mucho* and *varios* can sometimes take articles or determiners when they are placed before a noun:

- They can only take an article when the noun is followed by a complement:

  Los pocos amigos que tiene. *(The few friends he has.)*

  We cannot say **los pocos amigos* if *amigos* is not followed by something else, like *que tiene*.

- They can go with a possessive:

  sus pocos amigos *(his few friends)*

c) *Otro* can be used with any other determiner, except for numbers:

  el otro chico *(the other boy)*
  mi otro hermano *(my other brother)*
  Quiero este otro libro. *(I want this other book.)*

Unlike other languages, *otro* can never be used with the indefinite article (*un* with its inflected forms). This is why the construction **un otro chico* cannot be used.

d) *Cualquiera* does not take determiners or articles when it precedes a noun. However, it is commonly used as an adjective after a noun. When this occurs, you need to put the indefinite article before the noun:

cualquier día *(any day)*
un día cualquiera *(just any day)*

4.4.c. Agreement

First group

The members of the first group are not inflected. If an adjective, pronoun or other determiner appear in the same sentence, they take the masculine singular form when used with one of the indefinites in this group:

No vi a nadie cansado. *(I saw nobody tired.)*
Supongo que hay algo, pero yo no lo veo. *(I guess there is something, but I can't see it.)*

PRON & DET

Second group

The indefinites in the second series are always inflected to indicate a change in number and they are often inflected to indicate change in gender. When they are determiners, they must agree with the noun they accompany:

otro amigo *(another friend)*
otra amiga *(another friend)*
otros amigos *(other friends)*
otras amigas *(other friends)*

When they are pronouns, they also agree with the noun they replace, or the noun they refer to:

Quiero otro. *(I want another [one]. Where* otro *refers, for instance, to* lápiz, libro, helado, etc. *(pencil, book, ice cream).*
Quiero otra. *Where* otra *refers, for instance, to* goma, libreta, golosina etc. *(eraser, notebook, candy).*

4.5. Numerals

Numerals are used to indicate exact quantities. Their meaning is associated with natural numbers. Numerals are divided into several groups. The two main groups comprise cardinal numbers and ordinal numbers:

4. Pronouns and determiners

- Cardinal numbers express an exact number or quantity:

  Hay dos árboles en el jardín. *(There are two trees in the garden.)*
  El curso dura diez semanas. *(The academic course lasts ten weeks.)*

- Ordinal numbers express the position of a noun in a numerical series:

  Siempre le gusta llegar el primero. *(He always likes to arrive first.)*
  Lo conocí el tercer día. *(I met him on the third day.)*

There are other kinds of numerals that are not covered in this grammar book: multiplicative numerals, which indicate multiplication (*doble, triple,* etc.), and partitive numerals, which express an exact division or fraction (*la mitad, un tercio,* etc.).

4.5.a. Cardinal numbers

Cardinal numbers indicate an exact number or quantity.

Forms

The cardinal numbers in Spanish are as follows:

0	cero	16	dieciséis
1	un / uno, una	17	diecisiete
2	dos	18	dieciocho
3	tres	19	diecinueve
4	cuatro	20	veinte
5	cinco	21	veintiuno
6	seis	30	treinta
7	siete	31	treinta y uno
8	ocho	40	cuarenta
9	nueve	50	cincuenta
10	diez	60	sesenta
11	once	70	setenta
12	doce	80	ochenta
13	trece	90	noventa
14	catorce	100	cien
15	quince	101	ciento uno

200	doscientos, -as	900	novecientos, -as
300	trescientos, -as	1,000	mil
400	cuatrocientos, -as	1,001	mil uno
500	quinientos, -as	10,000	diez mil
600	seiscientos, -as	100,000	cien mil
700	setecientos, -as	1,000,000	un millón
800	ochocientos, -as		

Observations

It is important to study the following aspects closely:

● *Uno* is shortened to *un* when it precedes a masculine noun. However, the full form is used when it does not accompany a noun:

He comprado un libro. *(I bought one book.)*
He comprado tres libros, sólo uno en español. *(I bought three books, but only one in Spanish.)*

However, the form *una* is always used with feminine nouns:

He comprado una novela. *(I bought one novel.)*
He comprado tres novelas, sólo una en español. *(I bought three novels, but only one in Spanish.)*

The same rule applies to other numbers ending in *–uno*:

He comprado veintiún libros. *(I bought twenty-one books.)*
He comprado veintiuna novelas. *(I bought twenty-one novels.)*
Libros, he comprado veintiuno. *(Books… I bought twenty-one.)*
Novelas, he comprado veintiuna. *(Novels… I bought twenty-one.)*

● The numbers between 1 and 30 are written as one word:

cero, uno, dos, tres *(zero, one, two, three)*
diez, once, doce, trece *(ten, eleven, twelve, thirteen)*
veinte, veintiuno, veintidós *(twenty, twenty-one, twenty-two)*

The tens and units of the numbers between 30 and 99 are joined by the conjunction *y*:

treinta y uno, treinta y dos, *etc. (thirty-one, thirty-two)*

PRON & DET

4. Pronouns and determiners

This rule does not apply to cardinal numbers from one hundred upwards.

- The number 100 is *cien*. The form *ciento* is used for the numbers between 101 and 199. The form *ciento* and the number that follows it are not joined by the conjunction *y*:

ciento uno *(101)*
ciento dos *(102)*
ciento diecinueve *(119)*
ciento treinta y dos *(132)*

- The form *ciento* is not inflected to indicate a change in gender. However, the other hundreds are inflected:

ciento dos chicos *(one hundred and two boys)*
ciento dos chicas *(one hundred and two girls)*
doscientos chicos *(two hundred boys)*
doscientas chicas *(two hundred girls)*

- In Spanish, *un billón* is a million million, not a thousand million.

Collective nouns associated with numbers

In Spanish, there are some collective nouns that designate a specific number of units. For example, *diez libros (ten books)* and *una decena de libros (about ten books)* mean the same thing.

These nouns are listed below:

1	una unidad	Las coles se venden por unidades. *(Cabbages are sold by units.)*
2	un par / una pareja	Un par de calcetines *(A pair of socks)* Júntense por parejas. *(Get together in pairs.)*
3	un trío	Un trío de ases *(Three aces)*
10	una decena	Una decena de libros *(About ten books)*
12	una docena	Una docena de huevos *(A dozen eggs)*
15	una quincena	La primera quincena de marzo *(The first two weeks in March)*
20	una veintena	Una veintena de canales de TV *(About twenty TV channels)*
30	una treintena	Una treintena de alumnos *(About thirty students)*

40	una cuarentena	Una cuarentena de enfermos
		(About forty patients)
50	una cincuentena	Una cincuentena de policías
		(About fifty police officers)
100	un centenar /	Un centenar de seguidores
	una centena	*(About a hundred followers)*
1,000	un millar	Un millar de denuncias
		(About a thousand complaints)

Function of cardinal numbers

Cardinal numerals indicate an exact number or quantity and always refer to a noun. They can be used:

- As determiners, preceding the noun they accompany:

  Hay dos edificios de cinco plantas. *(There are two five-story buildings.)*

- As pronouns, replacing the noun:

  Hay tres. *(There are three.)*
  Tengo cinco. *(I have five.)*
  Los cinco son míos. *(All five are mine.)*
  He enviado cinco correos, pero sólo me han respondido tres. *(I sent five e-mails, but only three were answered.)*

As a rule, cardinal numbers cannot be placed after the noun they accompany, although they can follow a stressed personal pronoun:

  Nosotros tres ya lo sabíamos.
  Os lo dejaré sólo a vosotros dos.

When they follow a noun, they do not indicate the number of elements included in a group, but the position of the noun in a series. In other words, they are interpreted as an ordinal number:

  el capítulo quince *(chapter fifteen)*
  el piso veintidós *(floor number twenty-two)*

Agreement

Cardinal numbers are not usually inflected to indicate a change in gender or number, meaning that they do not agree with the noun they accompany:

4. Pronouns and determiners

> Hay **doce** chicos. *(There are twelve boys.)*
> Hay **doce** chicas. *(There are twelve girls.)*

- *Uno* and the numbers that include it always agree in gender with the noun:

> Hay un perro. *(There is one dog.)* Hay una perra.
> Hay veintiún perros. *(There are twenty-one dogs.)* Hay veintiuna perras.
> Perros, hay uno. *(Dogs… There's one.)* Perras, hay una.

However, the form *un* must be used before feminine nouns that begin with a stressed *a* or *ha*: treinta y un águilas (thirty-one eagles) (but not *treinta y una águilas)

- Multiples of *ciento* agree in gender with the noun:

> Vinieron doscientos chicos. *(Two hundred boys came.)*
> Vinieron doscientas chicas. *(Two hundred girls came.)*
> Contrataron cuatrocientos operarios. *(They hired four hundred workers.)*
> Contrataron cuatrocientas empleadas. *(They hired four hundred employees.)*

- The forms *cien* and *ciento* do not agree with the noun as they are not inflected to indicate a change in gender.

> Vinieron cien chicos. *(One hundred boys came.)*
> Vinieron cien chicas. *(One hundred girls came.)*
> Vinieron ciento cincuenta chicos. *(One hundred fifty boys came.)*
> Vinieron ciento cincuenta chicas. *(One hundred fifty girls came.)*

4.5.b. Ordinal numbers

Ordinal numbers express the position of something in a numerical series.

Forms

The ordinal numbers in Spanish are as follows:

1 st	primer / primero, primera, primeros, primeras
2 nd	segundo, segunda, segundos, segundas
3 rd	tercer / tercero, tercera, terceros, terceras
4 th	cuarto, cuarta, cuartos, cuartas
5 th	quinto, quinta, quintos, quintas
6 th	sexto, sexta, sextos, sextas
7 th	séptimo, séptima, séptimos, séptimas
8 th	octavo, octava, octavos, octavas

9 th	noveno, novena, novenos, novenas
10 th	décimo, décima, décimos, décimas
11 th	undécimo, undécima, undécimos, undécimas
12 th	duodécimo, duodécima, duodécimos, duodécimas
13 th	décimo tercero, décimo tercera, décimo terceros, décimo terceras
14 th	décimo cuarto, décimo cuarta, décimo cuartos, décimo cuartas
15 th	décimo quinto, décimo quinta, décimo quintos, décimo quintas
16 th	décimo sexto, décimo sexta, décimo sextos, décimo sextas
17 th	décimo séptimo, décimo séptima, décimo séptimos, décimo séptimas
18 th	décimo octavo, décimo octava, décimo octavos, décimo octavas
19 th	décimo noveno, décimo novena, décimo novenos, décimo novenas
20 th	vigésimo, vigésima, vigésimos, vigésimas
21 th	vigésimo primero, vigésimo primera, vigésimo primeros, vigésimo primeras
30 th	trigésimo, trigésima, trigésimos, trigésimas
40 th	cuadragésimo, cuadragésima, cuadragésimos, cuadragésimas
50 th	quincuagésimo, quincuagésima, quincuagésimos, quincuagésimas
60 th	sexagésimo, sexagésima, sexagésimos, sexagésimas
70 th	septuagésimo, septuagésima, septuagésimos, septuagésimas
80 th	octogésimo, octogésima, octogésimos, octogésimas
90 th	nonagésimo, nonagésima, nonagésimos, nonagésimas
100 th	centésimo, centésima, centésimos, centésimas
1,000 th	milésimo, milésima, milésimos, milésimas

PRON & DET

Observations

● It is important to note that when the forms *primero* and *tercero* precede a singular masculine noun the final -*o* is dropped:

el primer capítulo *(the first chapter)*
el tercer capítulo *(the third chapter)*

However, the full forms of *primero* and *tercero* are used before a feminine noun and when they are used pronominally:

la primera parte *(the first part)*
la tercera parte *(the third part)*
Los capítulos que me han gustado más son el primero y el tercero. *(I liked the first and third chapters best.)*

- Ordinal numbers between 1.º and 10.º are frequently used. However, they are seldom used for ordinals higher than 10.º In these cases, the cardinal number is used and placed after the noun:

  Vivo en el segundo piso. *(I live on the second floor.)*
  Vivo en el piso catorce. *(I live on floor number fourteen.)*

- The adjectives *último*, *penúltimo* and *antepenúltimo* have a very similar value to ordinal numbers. They indicate a position in a sequence of elements, but they are not numbers in the strict sense of the word because they do not indicate a numerical position.

Function of ordinal numerals

Ordinal numerals are generally used:

- Before the noun they accompany:

  Vivo en el cuarto piso. *(I live on the fourth floor.)*

- Without the noun when the meaning is inferred:

  Vivo en el cuarto. *(I live on the fourth.)*

Nevertheless, they can also be placed after the noun, although this usage is not as frequent:

  Vivo en el piso cuarto. *(I live on the fourth floor.)*

In all cases, the definite article is usually required.

Agreement

Ordinal numbers always agree in gender and number with the noun they accompany or replace:

  el primer corredor *(the first runner)*
  la primera corredora *(the first runner)*
  los primeros corredores *(the first runners)*
  las primeras corredoras *(the first runners)*

5. Relatives and interrogatives

Relatives are words that are used to introduce subordinate clauses that function as the complement of a noun. The words underlined in the following sentences are subordinate clauses that act as the complement of the noun *casa* and each of them is introduced by the relatives *la cual, donde* and *que*:

La casa de la cual te hablé está cerca del centro de la ciudad. *(The house I talked to you about, is near the center of the city.)*
La casa donde vive Pilar está cerca del centro de la ciudad. *(The house where Pilar lives, is near the center of the city.)*
La casa que me he comprado está cerca del centro de la ciudad. *(The house I bought is near the center of the city.)*

The words used to introduce these types of clauses are very similar in form and function to those used to make questions (interrogatives). The following questions are introduced by the interrogatives *cuál, dónde, qué* (which, where, what):

¿De cuál te hablé? *(Which one did I talked to you about?)*
¿Dónde vive Pilar? *(Where does Pilar live?)*
¿Qué casa me he comprado? *(What house did I buy?)*

From a grammatical viewpoint, relatives and interrogatives are divided into two groups: pronouns and adverbs. However, although they belong to different grammatical categories, they function in very similar ways. This is why we have brought them together in one chapter instead of dealing with them separately in the chapters on pronouns and adverbs.

5.1. Relatives

5.1.a. General questions

Relatives are connecting words that introduce a type of subordinate clause known as a relative clause. Relative clauses generally act as the complement of a noun.

5. Relatives and interrogatives

El estudiante que me presentaste ayer era simpático.
antecedent *subordinate*

In English, *The student you introduced to me yesterday was nice.*

The relative antecedent

The word or words that subordinate clauses modify are known as *antecedents*. In many cases, the antecedent of a subordinate clause is a noun, as occurs in the example above. These clauses can also take other antecedents. In the example below, the antecedent of the subordinate clause is the first part of the sentence:

Nos ha intentado engañar, lo cual nos ha disgustado mucho.
antecedent *subordinate*

In English, *He tried to cheat on us, and that has been very upsetting.*

On other occasions, the subordinate clause does not have an explicit antecedent. In these cases, it has a generic interpretation. In other words, it refers to any person or object with the characteristics indicated in the subordinate clause:

Quien hace poco deporte puede tener problemas de salud. *(Someone not doing enough exercise can have health problems.)*

In order to know which form of the relative to use, you first need to recognize its antecedent. This is because differences are often seen in the use of relatives depending on whether their antecedent is a noun or a clause, or whether they have an antecedent or not.

Types of subordinate clause

Subordinate clauses with a nominal antecedent can be classified into two types: explicative and specificative. They can be distinguished by the role they perform in the sentence:

- Specificative clauses restrict the object or person the antecedent refers to. In other words, a noun cannot refer to a single object or person on its own, but to a group. The relative clause specifies which object or person the antecedent specifically refers to.

For example, in the following sentence, the subordinate clause (which is specificative) allows us to identify which windows we are referring to:

those overlooking the street. It is inferred that there are other windows that do not overlook the street:

Entra mucha luz por las ventanas que dan a la calle. *(A lot of light comes in through the windows that open to the street.)*

- Explicatives provide information about the antecedent, but they do not restrict the group of elements the noun refers to:

For instance, in the following sentence, the subordinate clause does not establish a subgroup within the group of windows, but indicates that the only windows that exist overlook the street and let in a lot of light:

Entra mucha luz por las ventanas, que dan a la calle. *(A lot of light comes in through the windows that open to the street.)*

In spoken Spanish, explicative clauses are usually expressed by pauses in speech and, in written Spanish, they are usually separated by commas, unlike specificative clauses.

In Spanish, some relatives behave differently depending on the type of subordinate clause they are used in.

Prepositions and relatives

The relative performs a syntactical function within the subordinate clause it introduces. In order to recognize this function, the subordinate clause usually changes into a main clause in which the relative is replaced by its antecedent:

El libro que he leído. ⇒ He leído un libro.

In English, *The book that I have read.* ⇒ *I have read a book.*

The relative in the subordinate clause sometimes requires a preposition. In some languages, like English, this preposition usually appears within the subordinate clause, in the same position it would take in a main clause in which the relative would be replaced by its antecedent: *A book that we talk about.* ⇒ *We talk about a book.* However, in these cases in Spanish, the preposition must precede the relative pronoun and does not appear within the clause: *Un libro sobre el que hablamos (A book we talked about),* but not **un libro que hablamos sobre.*

5.1.b. Forms

There are two groups of relatives: pronouns and adverbs.

Relative pronouns

The relative pronouns are as follows:

PRONOUN	INFLECTED FORMS
que	que; el que / la que / lo que / los que / las que
quien	quien / quienes
cual	el cual / la cual / lo cual / los cuales / las cuales

The forms *cuanto* and *cuyo* are also relative pronouns. We are not going to deal with them in this grammar because their usage is very complex.

Relative pronouns are usually inflected to indicate a change in number and, in some cases, they are inflected to indicate a change in gender. Relatives agree in gender and number with their antecedent when they have the corresponding inflected forms. The relative forms, preceded by the neutral article *lo*, are used in clausal antecedents or in some cases of subordinate clauses without an explicit antecedent.

Relative adverbs

There are three kinds of relative adverbs in Spanish. Just like all adverbs, these forms are not inflected: *donde, cuando, como (where, when, as)*.

When relative adverbs form relative clauses they always take an explicit antecedent, which must be a noun. In other words, they can never form sentences without an antecedent or sentences with a clausal antecedent.

Relative adverbs can introduce adverbial clauses of place, time and manner:

Lo encontré donde lo había dejado. *(I found it where I left it.)*
Me alegré cuando lo supe. *(I was glad when I heard the news.)*
Lo resolví como pude. *(I solved it as I could.)*

5.1.c. Function

The general function of all relative pronouns and adverbs is to introduce subordinate clauses.

Que

This is the most widely used relative pronoun and adverb. It can be used in any kind of subordinate clause and with any kind of antecedent, and can also be preceded by any preposition:

> He visto la computadora que me quiero comprar. *(I saw the PC that I want to buy.)*
> El jugador, que estaba poco concentrado, perdió el partido. *(The player that was not concentrated enough lost the game.)*
> No sé qué esperas de mí, lo que me pone muy nervioso. *(I don't know what you are expecting from me, and that makes me very nervous.)*
> Un autor por el que siento una gran admiración. *(An author that I admire greatly.)*

Que is not inflected and, as a result, does not agree with its antecedent. It is sometimes preceded by the definite article. In these cases, the article agrees with the antecedent.

> El chico sobre el que te hablé. *(The boy that I talked to you about.)*
> La chica sobre la que te hablé. *(The girl that I talked to you about.)*

El / la / lo / los / las + que

The relative pronoun *que* can be used on its own, without a determiner, or preceded by the definite article. Both constructions can sometimes alternate in the same sentence. Sometimes, only one of them is possible.

The construction *definite article + que* is used in the following cases:

- In clauses with a specific antecedent, it is usually used when the relative is preceded by a preposition:

> El caso del que me han informado. *(The case that I was informed about.)*
> Una mujer sin la que no puedo vivir. *(A woman that I can't live without.)*

In this case, the article can be omitted.

- The article can never be omitted in clauses without an explicit antecedent:

> He visto muchas películas. La que más me gustó fue la de Almodóvar. *(I've seen many movies. The one that I liked best was Almodóvar's.)*
> El que lo sepa, que se calle. *(He who knows, should keep it to himself.)*

The construction *article + que* can be replaced by the relative pronoun *quien* or *quienes* when it refers to a person:

5. Relatives and interrogatives

Una mujer sin la que no puedo vivir. ⇒ Una mujer sin quien no puedo vivir.
(A woman that I can't live without / A woman without whom I can't live.)
El que lo sepa, que se calle. ⇒ Quien lo sepa, que se calle. *(He who knows,
should keep it to himself. / Who ever knows it, should keep it to himself.)*

The form *lo que* is a special case of a construction with the definite article that often causes problems for learners of Spanish. It is used in the following cases:

- In clauses without an explicit antecedent, when the clause refers to something that is not specified or is not known. In these cases, the relative pronoun can be replaced by *una cosa que*, *eso que* or a similar structure:

  Me has traído lo que te pedí. *(You brought me what I asked for.)*
  It can be replaced by aquella cosa que te pedí: Me has traído aquella cosa que te
  pedí. *(You brought me that thing I asked you for.)*

- In clauses without an explicit antecedent, when the relative clause refers to an idea, a situation or an event, and not a specific object:

  Lo que ocurre es que estoy cansado. *(What happens is that I'm tired.)*

- When the explicit or implicit antecedent is part of a separate clause:

  Ninguno de los tres ha puesto la mesa, *lo que* me parece una grosería. *(None of
  the three has set the table, which seems very rude to me.)*
  ¿Puedes repetir lo que has dicho, por favor? *(Can you please repeat what you
  said?)*

  In these cases, *lo que* can sometimes by replaced by the interrogative pronoun *qué*:

  Cuéntame lo que sabes. *(Tell me what you know.)*
  Cuéntame qué sabes. *(Tell me what you know.)*

Quien, quienes

This relative pronoun only introduces subordinate clauses when the explicit or implicit antecedent is a person. It can always be replaced by *el/la/los/las + que*.

The relative pronoun *quien* or *quienes* cannot be used in all the cases when the antecedent is a person, but only in these two cases:

- When the pronoun is preceded by a preposition:

  El hombre a quien conocimos. *(The man who we met.)*

- When there is no explicit antecedent:

    Quien lo quiera ver, puede venir. *(Anyone who wants to see it, can come.)*

Cual, cuales

The relative pronoun *cual* or *cuales* is used to replace *que, quien* or *quienes*. Both sets of pronouns are interchangeable and, in some cases, the use of one or another depends on stylistic factors. For instance, *cual* is more formal.

This relative pronoun is always preceded by the definite article. It can only be used:

- When it is preceded by a preposition:

    El motivo por el cual he venido… *(The reason that I have come…)*

- Without a preposition, in explicative clauses. It is never used in specificative clauses:

    Las causas del accidente, el cual se podría haber evitado, están siendo investigadas. *(The causes of the accident, which could have been avoided, are being investigated.)*

The form preceded by the neutral article, *lo cual*, is used with a clausal antecedent:

El presidente del gobierno afirmó que había bajado los impuestos, lo cual es falso. *(The prime minister said that he had reduced taxes, which is false.)*

Relative adverbs: *donde, cuando* and *como*

The relative adverbs *donde, cuando, como* *(where, when, how)* are used in subordinate clauses with antecedents indicating place, time and manner.

- *Donde* and *como* are used very frequently.

    El lugar donde lo has escondido. *(The place where you hid it.)*
    El modo como nos lo contó. *(It was the way how she told us.)*

    Donde can be replaced by *en que* or *en el que*:

    El lugar donde lo has escondido. *(The place where you hid it.)*
    El lugar en que lo has escondido. *(The place where (in which) you hid it.)*

● However, *cuando* is seldom used with an explicit antecedent. The construction preposition + *el que o que* is used in its place:

El momento cuando lo supimos.
(The moment when we found out.)

El momento en el que lo supimos.
(The moment when (in which) we found out.)

The same adverbs are used to introduce subordinate clauses without an explicit antecedent. These are not relative clauses.

Iremos donde nos apetezca.
(We'll go where we please.)
Me gusta la playa cuando hace buen tiempo.
(I like the beach when there's good weather.)
He cocinado la carne como te gusta.
(I cooked the meat as you like it.)

5.2. Interrogatives

Interrogatives are words used to make questions. They always appear at the start of the sentence.

¿Dónde estás? *(Where are you?)*
¿Quién es aquel chico? *(Who is that boy?)*
¿Qué quieres? *(What do you want?)*

They can also be used to introduce exclamatory clauses:

¡Qué bien nos lo hemos pasado! *(We had a lot of fun!)*

Interrogative forms are very similar to relative forms but, unlike them, they are always stressed and written with an accent.

5.2.a. Forms

Like relatives, interrogatives are divided into two groups: pronouns and adverbs.

Interrogative pronouns

The interrogative pronouns in Spanish are as follows. Some of them are inflected to indicate a change in number and gender:

qué	qué
quién	quién / quiénes
cuál	cuál / cuáles
cuánto	cuánto / cuánta / cuántos / cuántas

The inflected forms must agree in number and gender with the noun they refer to.

Interrogative adverbs

There are three interrogative adverbs: *dónde, cuándo, cómo* (where?, when?, how?). Just like all adverbs, they are not inflected and, therefore, do not agree.

5.2.b. Function

Interrogative adverbs can perform two functions: they can be used to form questions or to express exclamations:

> ¿Qué haces? *(What are you doing?)*
> ¡Qué bonito! *(How nice!)*

They can also introduce a subordinate clause with an interrogative sense that depends on a verb of communication (such as *decir, preguntar [to say, to ask]*) or a verb of knowledge (such as *saber, ignorar, conocer [to know, to ignore, to know]*):

> Pregunta quién lo ha hecho. *(Ask who did it.)*
> No sé quién lo ha hecho. *(I don't know who did it.)*

When they introduce a direct question, or a question in a subordinate clause, they can be preceded by a preposition:

> ¿De qué me hablas? *(What are you talking about?)*
> No sé de dónde ha venido. *(I don't know where he has come from.)*

Just like relatives, prepositions that perform an interrogative function must precede the interrogative adverb. They cannot be placed next to the verb: *¿De dónde eres? (Where are you from?)* [but not *¿Dónde eres de?*].

The usage of interrogatives in Spanish is different from other languages, such as English.

Each interrogative adverb is used in a specific type of question.

5. Relatives and interrogatives

Qué

It is used to ask about objects and things, but not about people:

¿Qué quieres? *(What do you want?)*

Quién and *quiénes*

They are used to ask about people:

¿Quién ha hecho esto? *(Who has done this?)*

The plural form is not used very often because the singular form can be used instead, even though we assume the answer will be plural. In other words, the previous question does not necessary imply that the answer will refer to just one person, but can include more than one person; for instance, Juan and María.

Cuál, cuáles

This pronoun (singular and plural) can be used in questions about objects and people:

De mis primos, ¿cuál te parece más simpático? *(Which one of my cousins seems nicest to you?)*
De los cuentos que leímos, ¿cuáles te gustaron más? *(Of the stories we read, which you liked best?)*

Cuál and *qué / quién* are not interchangeable: *cuál* is used to ask about an object or person within a group or class that is known about or mentioned. For instance, in the previous sentences, "mis primos" and "los cuentos".

It is important to know that some constructions always require *cuál* or *qué*:

● *Cuál* + verb *ser* + noun:

¿Cuál es la película que más te ha gustado? *(Which movie did you like best?)*
[*but not* *¿Qué es la película…?].

● *Cuál* + *de* + (determiner) noun:

¿Cuál de estos libros es más entretenido? *(Which of these books is most entertaining?)* [*but not* *¿Qué de estos libros…?].

● *Qué* + noun:

¿Qué profesor te gusta más? *(Which professor do you like best?)*
[*but not* *¿Cuál profesor…?].

Cuánto, cuánta, cuántos, cuántas

These are used to ask about quantities. They can be accompanied by the noun that indicates the class of objects whose quantity we are asking about, or without a noun, which it replaces:

> ¿Cuántos quieres? *(How many do you want?)*
> ¿Cuántos amigos tienes? *(How many friends do you have?)*

This pronoun must always agree in gender and number with the noun it accompanies or replaces:

> ¿Cuántos chicos hay en la clase? *(How many boys are there in the classroom?)*
> ¿Cuántas chicas hay en la clase? *(How many girls are there in the classroom?)*

In the singular, it can only be used with uncountable nouns:

> ¿Cuánto dinero tienes? *(How much money do you have?)*
> ¿Cuánto arroz hay que poner en la sopa? *(How much rice should we add to the soup?)*

Interrogative adverbs: *dónde, cuándo* and *cómo*

Interrogative adverbs are used to ask about a place, time or manner:

> ¿Dónde está Madrid? *(Where is Madrid?)*
> ¿Cuándo llegará el avión de Nueva York? *(When is the flight from New York arriving?)*
> ¿Cómo se hace esto? *(How can you do this?)*

REL &
INTRR

6. Verbs

Verbs in Spanish are inflected. This means that the same verb has different forms depending on the tense or certain grammatical questions, such as agreement. For instance, in the following sentences, the form of the verb changes to express different tenses:

Daniel habla con María. *(Daniel talks with María.)*
Daniel habló con María. *(Daniel talked with María.)*
Daniel hablaba con María. *(Daniel was talking with María.)*
Daniel hablará con María. *(Daniel will talk with María.)*

The different tenses in Spanish are expressed by the inflection of the verb. This means that to use a verb correctly in Spanish you have to know how to conjugate the different verb forms and what part of the verb they represent.

6.1. Conjugation

The variation of the form of a verb is known as *conjugation*. In other words, the conjugation of a verb includes all the forms of a verb in all its tenses.

6.1.a. Forming tenses

The forms of conjugation of a verb vary according to two factors: the person and number, and the tense it is used in.

Agreement: person and number

The form of the verb depends on its subject. For example, in the sentences below, the form of the verb changes because the subject changes:

Yo canto. *(I sing.)*
Tú cantas. *(You sing.)*
Él canta. *(He sings.)*

In other words, in Spanish, the verb agrees with the subject of the sentence. Agreement takes place according to the different grammatical traits: the grammatical person and number.

- The grammatical person depends on whether the subject is the speaker, the addressee or a third party:

> **First person:** *the subject agrees with the speaker / speakers:* yo / nosotros, nosotras
>
> **Second person:** *the subject agrees with the person / people being spoken to:* tú / vosotros, vosotras
>
> **Third person:** *the subject is someone who is neither the speaker nor the addressee:* él, ella / ellos, ellas.

- The number depends on whether the subject is singular or plural:

Singular: El coche corre mucho. *(The car runs fast.)*
Plural: Los coches corren mucho. *(The cars run fast.)*

This means that Spanish verbs have six different conjugated forms: three for the singular (first, second and third person) and three for the plural.

Tenses

Verbs also vary according to the tense they express. For example, in the two sentences below, the first one expresses an action taking place in the past, whereas the second expresses an action in the future:

El equipo de fútbol ganó el partido. *(The soccer team won the game.)*
El equipo de fútbol ganará el partido. *(The soccer team will win the game.)*

Spanish verbs can express many different tense values, with differences that are sometimes not expressed in other languages. In the examples below, the two sentences express an action in the past. However, in the first one the action had been completed at the time of speaking, whereas, in the second, the action was still happening at the time of speaking:

El niño leyó un libro. *(The boy read a book.)*
El niño leía un libro. *(The boy was reading a book.)*

This means that the conjugation of verbs involves many different tenses that express different tense values. To know which form of verb to use, it is important to know which tense value you want to express and how to form the corresponding tense.

VRB

6.1.b. Verbal inflection

The different conjugated forms of a verb are obtained through inflection. This means that, with some exceptions, all the conjugated forms share the same root or stem which remains unchanged in every tense. Different endings are added to this root according to the values of the person and number, and the tense: *cant – o, cant – aba, cant – aste*.

Not all verbs take the same endings to form the conjugated tenses. Verbs are classified into three main groups according to the endings they take. These groups of verbs are known as *conjugations*. There are three conjugations that can be recognized by the ending they take in the infinitive:

> **First conjugation** (–ar): cantar, pensar, amar, saltar, jugar
> **Second conjugation** (–er): beber, temer, soler, ser, poder, tejer
> **Third conjugation** (–ir): vivir, partir, pedir, conducir, venir

With few exceptions, the verbs that belong to each of these three conjugations make up the different verbal tenses that use the same endings.

6.1.c. Simple and compound tenses

Verbal tenses are divided into simple and compound tenses, depending on the way they are formed:

- Simple tenses are formed by adding the corresponding endings to the root of the verb being conjugated: *canto, canté, cantaba*.

- Compound tenses are formed with the verb *haber*, conjugated in a verbal tense, followed by the participle of the verb being conjugated: *he cantado, había cantado, habré cantado*.

6.1.d. Regular and irregular verbs

Most Spanish verbs are conjugated, with their different persons and numbers, by adding the corresponding endings to the root of the verb. The root remains unchanged and the same endings are used for all other verbs in the same conjugation. These verbs are known as **regular** verbs.

However, a few verbs change their root or stem during conjugation. This can occur when one of the inflected forms alternates with the root of the verb.

For example:

podemos – puedo – pudo
conozco – conoce
pongo – pones – puso

Certain tense forms take different endings than other verbs in the same conjugation: *hay, soy, voy…*

The verbs that take different endings to the other model verbs, or change their root, are called **irregular** verbs.

Below, follows an explanation of how the most common verbal tenses are formed in Spanish. It also lists the most frequent irregularities that occur in these tenses, and shows the most common values and uses of these tenses. This chapter does not include all the possible verbal tenses in Spanish. It only deals with the forms that are suitable for a grammar of this level.

6.2. The present indicative (*presente de indicativo*)

The present indicative is used to express an action in progress at the time of speaking.

Luis conduce hacia Murcia. *(Luis drives to Murcia.)*
María está en el médico. *(María is at the doctor's.)*
El niño come. *(The boy eats.)*

VRB

6.2.a. Conjugation

Regular verbs

The present indicative of regular verbs in Spanish is formed by adding the following endings to each conjugation:

	1st conj. (*–ar*)	2nd conj. (*–er*)	3rd conj. (*–ir*)
yo	cant – o	beb – o	viv – o
tú	cant – as	beb – es	viv – es
el / ella	cant – a,	beb – e	viv – e
nosotros/-as	cant – amos	beb – emos	viv – imos
vosotros/-as	cant – áis,	beb – éis	viv – ís
ellos/ellas	cant – an	beb – en	viv – en

Irregular verbs

Most Spanish verbs form the present indicative according to the regular model. Nevertheless, there are some irregular verbs in the present indicative. The main groups of present-tense irregular verbs are listed below.

Radical changes

The root of the verb ends in the vowel *e / o*, which changes to another vowel or a diphthong in all the forms of the present, except for the first and second person plural. The verbs that have this type of irregularity are also irregular in the imperative.

The following three vowel changes take place with the verbs below:

e ⇒ ie	**querer** *(to love / to want)*: quiero, quieres, quiere, queremos, queréis, quieren *Other verbs:* *1st conj.:* acertar, cerrar, pensar, empezar, atravesar, despertar, merendar, regar, sentar, sentir, gobernar, temblar, *etc.* *2nd conj.:* entender, perder, tener, encender, etc.
e ⇒ i	**pedir** *(to ask for)*: pido, pides, pide, pedimos, pedís, piden *Other verbs:* *3rd conj.:* conseguir, corregir, despedir, elegir, medir, repetir, seguir, perseguir, servir, reír, vestir, *etc.*
o ⇒ ue	**poder** *(can / may)*: puedo, puedes, puede, podemos, podéis, pueden *Other verbs:* *1st conj.:* contar, soltar, encontrar, sonar, costar, recordar, volar, etc. *Notice that the verb jugar has a similar irregular form to this one, although in this case the u alternates with ue: juego, juegas, juega, jugamos, jugáis, juegan* *2nd conj.:* morder, volver, mover, *etc.* *3rd conj.:* dormir

Radical changes in verbs ending in –uir

In verbs ending in –*uir*, –*ui*– changes to –*uy*– in all the present forms, except for the first- and second-person plural. These verbs have the same type of irregularity in the imperative.

ui ⇒ uy	**huir**: huyo, huyes, huye, huimos, huís, huyen
	Other verbs: incluir, sustituir, construir, destruir, influir, distribuir, etc.

Consonant changes in the first-person singular

Some verbs display an irregularity in the present indicative that only affects the first-person singular. These irregularities lead to a change in the consonants that form the root of the verb, either because a consonant is added to the root or because one consonant changes to another. In some cases (for example with verbs like *escoger*), this change only affects the way the verb is written, but not the way it is pronounced. However, in most cases, the pronunciation changes.

The most common verbs with this irregularity are:

g ⇒ j	**escoger:** escojo, escoges, escoge, escogemos, escogéis, escogen
c ⇒ zc	**conducir:** conduzco, conduces, conduce, conducimos, conducís, conducen
	conocer: conozco, conoces, conoce, conocemos, conocéis, conocen
	parecer: parezco, pareces, parece, parecemos, parecéis, parecen
c ⇒ g	**hacer:** hago, haces, hace, hacemos, hacéis, hacen
Ø ⇒ g	**poner:** pongo, pones, pone, ponemos, ponéis, ponen
	salir: salgo, sales, sale, salimos, salís, salen
	traer: traigo, traes, trae, traemos, traéis, traen

There are also three frequently used verbs that are only irregular in the first-person singular. This irregularity is somewhat different to the ones listed above. The verbs are as follows:

dar	doy, das, da, damos, dais, dan
estar	estoy, estás, está, estamos, estáis, están
saber	sé, sabes, sabe, sabemos, sabéis, saben

Special irregular forms in commonly used verbs

Finally, there is a series of commonly used verbs that display a number of irregularities that affect different persons in the present indicative. They are either characteristic irregularities of this verb or the combination of more than one of the irregular forms mentioned above.

Below, you will find the conjugations of some of the most common irregular verbs in the present indicative which are important to learn.

ir	voy, vas, va, vamos, vais, van
venir	vengo, vienes, viene, venimos, venís, vienen
decir	digo, dices, dice, decimos, decís, dicen
tener	tengo, tienes, tiene, tenemos, tenéis, tienen
oír	oigo, oyes, oye, oímos, oís, oyen
ser	soy, eres, es, somos, sois, son

6.2.b. Use of the present

The present indicative is mainly used to express an action taking place at the time of speaking.

> Busco la raqueta de tenis. *(I am looking for the tenis racket.)*
> Juan hace la cama. *(Juan makes his bed.)*

The present indicative also has other uses:

- It enables us to talk about habitual actions, actions that are repeated or occur regularly over a period of time (in the past, present or future):

> Juego al ajedrez cada semana. *(I play chess every week.)*
> Trabajo en la televisión. *(I work on television.)*
> Todos los días como fruta. *(I eat fruit each day.)*
> No fumo. *(I don't smoke.)*

- It is used to talk about general truths that are considered universal. In other words, it is the tense we use to generalize. This usage is widespread in scientific language, in definitions, in sayings…:

  El Sol sale por el Este. *(The Sun rises in the east.)*
  Los delfines son mamíferos. *(Dolphins are mammals.)*
  Caminar es bueno para la salud. *(Walking is good for your health.)*

- It is sometimes used to express actions that will take place in the future but which are perceived as near or certain to happen:

  ¿Qué haces este verano? *(What are you doing this summer?)*
  En junio acabo la carrera. *(I will finish college in June.)*
  En septiembre me pongo a buscar trabajo. *(I will start looking for work in September.)*

6.3. Past tenses

The past tenses refer to an action that took place before the time of speaking.

Spanish has a number of past tenses. The difference between them largely depends on the following two factors:

- If we are referring to a moment in the distant past, not related to the time of speaking, or to a moment that has some connection with the present.

- If the action had finished or was still continuing at the time we are talking about.

6.3.a. The preterite tense (*pretérito indefinido*)

The preterite is a past tense that expresses actions that were completed in the past, or events that occurred at a specific time in the past.

Hace dos años fueron de vacaciones a Irlanda. *(Two years ago, they went to Ireland on vacation.)*
Los padres de Ana tuvieron tres hijos. *(Ana's parents had three children.)*
Su primer trabajo fue en Roma. *(Her first job was in Rome.)*

Conjugation

Regular verbs

Spanish verbs take the following endings to form the preterite tense, according to the conjugation they belong to:

VRB

6. Verbs

	1st conj. (–ar)	2nd conj. (–er)	3rd conj. (–ir)
yo	cant – é	beb – í	viv – í
tú	cant – aste	beb – iste	viv – iste
el / ella	cant – ó,	beb – ió	viv – ió
nosotros/–as	cant – amos	beb – imos	viv – imos
vosotros/–as	cant – asteis,	beb – isteis	viv – isteis
ellos/ellas	cant – aron	beb – ieron	viv – ieron

Irregular verbs

The main irregularities in the preterite tense can be classified into the two groups listed below.

- The third-person singular and plural of some verbs are irregular because the vowels of their stems change. In some, the vowel e changes to i, as is the case with the verb *pedir*. The vowel of the stem of other verbs is combined with the letter *y*, such as *leer* and *huir*. These changes are shown in the table below:

e ⇒ i	**pedir** *(to ask for)*: pedí, pediste, pidió, pedimos, pedisteis, pidieron
	Other verbs:
	3rd conj.: conseguir, corregir, despedir, elegir, medir, mentir, repetir, seguir, sentir, perseguir, servir, vestir, *etc.*
e ⇒ ey	**leer** *(to read)*: leí, leíste, leyó, leímos, leísteis, leyeron
	Other verbs:
	2nd conj.: verbs ending in the sequence vowel + er: creer, caer, etc.
u ⇒ uy	**huir** *(to flee / to escape)*: huí, huiste, huyó, huimos, huisteis, huyeron
	Other verbs:
	3rd conj.: verbs ending in –uir: incluir, sustituir, construir, destruir, reconstruir, influir, distribuir, etc.

- The preterite tense of some commonly used verbs is formed by using a different root to the one used to form other tenses. The verbs with these irregularities form the first- and third-person singular of the preterite tense by using different endings: with regular verbs, the first and third persons take an accent on the last letter (*corrió, comió,* etc.).

The main verbs with this type of irregularity are as follows:

Verb	Root + preterite tense
andar	**anduv–**: anduve, anduviste, anduvo, anduvimos, anduvisteis, anduvieron
caber	**cup–**: cupe, cupiste, cupo, cupimos, cupisteis, cupieron
dar	**di–**: di, diste, dio, dimos disteis, dieron
decir	**dij–**: dije, dijiste, dijo, dijimos, dijisteis, dijeron
estar	**estuv–**: estuve, estuviste, estuvo, estuvimos, estuvisteis, estuvieron
haber	**hub–**: hube, hubiste, hubo, hubimos, hubisteis, hubieron
hacer	**hic–**: hice, hiciste, hizo, hicimos, hicisteis, hicieron
ir	**fu–**: fui, fuiste, fue, fuimos, fuisteis, fueron
poder	**pud–**: pude, pudiste, pudo, pudimos, pudisteis, pudieron
poner	**pus–**: puse, pusiste, puso, pusimos, pusisteis, pusieron
querer	**quis–**: quise, quisiste, quisimos, quisisteis, quisieron
saber	**sup–**: supe, supiste, supo, supimos, supisteis, supieron
ser	**fu–**: fui, fuiste, fue, fuimos, fuisteis, fueron
tener	**tuv–**: tuve, tuviste, tuvo, tuvimos, tuvisteis, tuvieron
traer	**traj–**: traje, trajiste, trajo, trajimos, trajisteis, trajeron
venir	**vin–**: vine, viniste, vino, vinimos, vinisteis, vinieron
ver	**vi–**: vi, viste, vio, vimos, visteis, vieron

VRB

Use of the preterite tense

The preterite tense is used to express actions in the past with the following two characteristics:

- These actions are not included in the same unit of time (day, week, year, etc.) as the present. This tense contrasts with the present perfect tense (*pretérito perfecto*).

- The action has concluded at the time we are talking about, it is not continuing. This enables us to contrast this tense with the imperfect tense (*pretérito imperfecto*).

6. Verbs

El jueves encontré a Jaime al salir del cine. *(Thursday, I came across Jaime coming out from the movies.)*
Ayer fuimos al teatro. *(We went to the theater yesterday.)*

On many occasions, we use the preterite tense with past-time markers:

- Time markers that place the action at some time in the past:

  En 1939 acabó la Guerra Civil española. *(The Spanish Civil War ended in 1939.)*
  Juana murió hace dos años. *(Juana died two years ago.)*
  Ayer perdí las gafas de sol. *(I lost my sun glasses yesterday.)*

- Time markers that indicate how long an action lasted:

  De niño viví tres años en México. *(I lived three years in Mexico when I was a child.)*
  Viví durante dos meses en Londres. *(I lived two months in London.)*

- Time markers that indicate the end of the action:

  Estuve despierto hasta las 3 de la madrugada. *(I was awake until three in the morning.)*
  Viajó mucho hasta que se casó. *(She traveled a lot until she got married.)*
  Vivió con sus padres hasta que se fue a estudiar al extranjero. *(She lived with her parents until she went to study abroad.)*

The preterite tense is also used in the following cases:

- To express sequences of completed consecutive past actions:

  Cuando acabó los estudios, se fue a París. *(She went to Paris when she finished her studies.)*
  Después de comprar la casa, cambiamos el parquet, pintamos y compramos muebles. *(After buying the house, we changed the parquet flooring, painted (the walls), and bought (new) furniture.)*

- To refer to a completed period in the past as a whole:

  Las vacaciones fueron fantásticas. *(Our vacation was fantastic.)*
  El curso pasado me lo pasé muy bien. *(I enjoyed very much the past school year.)*

6.3.b. The imperfect tense (*pretérito imperfecto*)

The imperfect tense describes past actions at the time they were happening, or indicates that they were in the process of happening in the past. In other words, it emphasizes the continuation of an action in the past.

Nos conocimos cuando vivíamos en Escocia. *(We met when we were living in Scotland.)*
De pequeña quería ser astronauta. *(When I was a child, I wanted to be an astronaut.)*
Juan por aquel entonces tenía el pelo largo. *(Juan had long hair then.)*

Conjugation

Regular verbs

The imperfect tense has practically no irregular verbs. It is formed by adding the following endings to the stem, according to the conjugation of the verb:

	1st conj. (–ar)	2nd conj. (–er)	3rd conj. (–ir)
yo	cant – aba	beb – ía	viv – ía
tú	cant – abas	beb – ías	viv – ías
el / ella	cant – aba	beb – ía	viv – ía
nosotros/–as	cant – ábamos	beb – íamos	viv – íamos
vosotros/–as	cant – abais,	beb – íais	viv – íais
ellos/ellas	cant – aban	beb – ían	viv – ían

Irregular verbs

There are only three irregular verbs in the imperfect tense: *ser (to be)*, *ir (to go)* and *ver (to see)*.

They are conjugated as follows:

ser	era, eras, era, éramos, erais, eran
ir	iba, ibas, iba, íbamos, ibais, iban
ver	veía, veías, veía, veíamos, veíais, veían

Use of the imperfect tense

The imperfect tense describes past actions that were taking place at the time we are talking about or over an extended period of time:

En aquel entonces, estaba de moda llevar el pelo largo. *(At that time, it was fashionable to have long hair.)*
Cuando regresaba a casa, tropecé y me rompí la pierna. *(When I was returning home, I stumbled and broke a leg.)*

VRB

6. Verbs

Recuerdo muy bien que aquel día llovía mucho. *(I remember very well it was raining a lot that day.)*

The imperfect tense also has two other uses:

- It is used to describe people, things or events in the past:

  La casa era grande, pero tenía el jardín descuidado. *(The house was large, but it had a neglected garden.)*
  De niña, yo era inquieta y curiosa, y adoraba a mi padre. *(When I was a child, I was restless, curious and adored my father.)*

- It is used to talk about habitual or repeated actions in the past:

  Todas las tardes leía el periódico. *(He read the paper every evening.)*
  Cuando vivía en Londres iba a menudo a correr. *(I went jogging often when I was living in London.)*

6.3.c. The present perfect (*pretérito perfecto*)

The present perfect is used to talk about recent past actions that are in some way associated with the present or have some relevance to the present and have been completed at the time of speaking:

Hoy se han levantado a las seis de la mañana. *(They got up today at six in the morning.)*
Ya he terminado las correcciones. *(I have already finished proofreading.)*
Esta semana hemos acabado de planear las vacaciones. *(This week, we finished planning our vacation.)*

This tense is seldom used in Latin American Spanish.

Conjugation

The present perfect is a compound tense formed by the present tense of the auxiliary verb *haber* followed by the past participle:

	1st conj. (–ar)	2nd conj. (–er)	3rd conj. (–ir)
yo	he cantado	he bebido	he vivido
tú	has cantado	has bebido	has vivido
el / ella	ha cantado	ha bebido	ha vivido
nosotros/–as	hemos cantado	hemos bebido	hemos vivido
vosotros/–as	habéis cantado	habéis bebido	habéis vivido
ellos/ellas	han cantado	han bebido	han vivido

The only irregularities that exist in the formation of this tense concern the past participle. Some verbs have irregular past participles as explained in section 6.7.b. of this chapter.

Use of the present perfect

The present perfect is mainly used to talk about actions in the recent past that have some connection with the present. Unlike the preterite, the action takes place within the same unit of time (day, week, month, year, etc.) as the present.

Esta semana he llegado cada día tarde a clase. *(This week, I have been late to class every day.)*
Hoy he venido andando. *(I came walking today.)*

VRB

The present perfect is used with time expressions such as *esta semana, este mes, este año*, etc.:

Este año ha acabado su investigación. *(He has finished his research project this year.)*

● It is also used for actions that have taken place during the course of the day (when we are speaking on that same day) and is combined with time expressions such as *hoy, ahora, hace un rato*, etc.:

Hoy he comido legumbres. *(Today, I had vegetables.)*
Lo he perdido hace un rato. *(I lost it a while ago.)*

When used without a time expression, it usually refers to an action that has taken place at an unspecified time during the course of the day (when we are speaking on that same day):

6. Verbs

No sé dónde he dejado las gafas. *(I don't know where I have left my glasses.)*
¿Dónde has puesto las llaves? *(Where did you put the keys?)*

● We use time expressions such as *siempre, nunca, alguna vez*, to refer to actions that have taken place over a longer period of time or during a person's life:

Nunca he conseguido entender cómo funciona esta máquina. *(I have never managed to understand how this machine works.)*

The present perfect can also be used to express the causes of a present situation:

Llega pronto porque ha cogido un tren antes de lo habitual. *(She's arriving early because she took a train before her usual time.)*
Los pisos son más baratos que antes porque han bajado los precios debido a la crisis. *(Apartments are cheaper than before because prices have dropped on account of the crisis.)*

6.3.d. The past perfect (*pretérito pluscuamperfecto*)

The past perfect is the tense used to talk about something that had already happened at the time we are talking about:

Antes de salir de casa ya había preparado la comida. *(I had already prepared lunch before leaving home.)*
Cuando fue a hablar con él, su hija ya le había explicado la situación. *(When she went to talk to him, his daughter had already explained the situation.)*

Conjugation

The past perfect is a compound tense formed by the imperfect tense of the auxiliary verb *haber* followed by the past participle:

	1st conj. (–ar)	2nd conj. (–er)	3rd conj. (–ir)
yo	había cantado	había bebido	había vivido
tú	habías cantado	habías bebido	habías vivido
el / ella	había cantado	había bebido	había vivido
nosotros/–as	habíamos cantado	habíamos bebido	habíamos vivido
vosotros/–as	habíais cantado	habíais bebido	habíais vivido
ellos/ellas	habían cantado	habían bebido	habían vivido

The only irregularities that exist in the formation of this tense concern the past participle. Some verbs have irregular past participles as explained in section 6.7.b. of this chapter.

Use of the past perfect

The past perfect is used when a past action was completed before another action in the past:

> Cuando conocí a Sofía, ya había ido a Londres en dos ocasiones. *(When I met Sofía, she had already traveled to London twice.)*
> Ya le había explicado todo cuando me enteré de su situación. *(I had already explained everything when I found out about her situation.)*

This means that it allows us to explain the causes of a past action:

> —¿Por qué no fuiste a buscarle? *(Why didn't you go and look for him?)*
> —Porque no había acabado el examen. *(Because I had not finished the exam.)*

6.3.e. Contrasts between the past tenses

It is essential to look at the differences between some of the tenses in order to ensure you use the correct past tense in Spanish. The main confusion between tenses for learners of Spanish occurs with the preterite and imperfect tenses, and the preterite and present perfect.

Preterite tense and imperfect tense

The main differences between these tenses are as follows:

The preterite is used to refer to an action that was completed at some time in the past or at the time we are talking about.

The imperfect is used to refer to an action that was taking place at the time we are talking about.

- The preterite tense expresses an action that has finished at the time of speaking:

> Cuando regresé a casa, perdí las llaves. *(When I returned home, I lost the keys.)*

The moment we are talking about "I lost the keys".

The action of 'returning home' ends before the precise moment we are talking about. In other words, the keys were lost at home.

6. Verbs

- The imperfect tense expresses an action or situation that was ongoing at the precise moment we are talking about:

Cuando regresaba a casa, perdí las llaves. *(When I was returning home, I lost the keys.)*

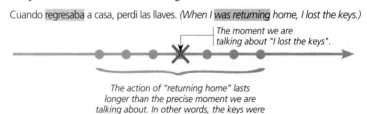

The moment we are talking about "I lost the keys".

The action of "returning home" lasts longer than the precise moment we are talking about. In other words, the keys were lost on the way home.

There is a second difference between these tenses, namely whether the action is repeated habitually or not:

Imperfect tense	Preterite tense
Habitual past actions that are repeated:	An action taking place at a specific time in the past that is not repeated:
De pequeño estaba muy enfermo. *(Habitual action: I was often ill.)*	De pequeño estuve muy enfermo. *(Specific action: I was very ill only once.)*

Preterite tense and present perfect tense

The main difference between the preterite and present perfect is whether the moment when the action took place is associated with the present or not.

- The preterite tense expresses actions that took place within a unit of time prior to the present unit of time:

El año pasado nos mudamos al piso nuevo. *(We moved to the new apartment last year.)*

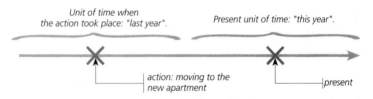

Unit of time when the action took place: "last year".

Present unit of time: "this year".

action: moving to the new apartment

present

- In the case of the present perfect, the action takes place within the same unit of time (day, week, month, year, etc.) as the present. The unit of time encompasses them both:

Este año nos **hemos mudado** al piso nuevo. *(We **moved** this year to the new apartament.)*

Unit of time "this year".

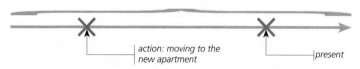

action: moving to the new apartment

present

6.4. Future tenses

The future tenses are used to refer to actions or events that have not yet happened.

6.4.a. The simple future (*futuro simple*)

This is the tense used to talk about future actions or events:

Mañana **comeré** en casa. *(I **will lunch** at home tomorrow.)*
Pronto **sabremos** a quién le han concedido la beca. *(We **will** soon **know** who got the scholarship.)*

VRB

Conjugation

Regular verbs

In Spanish, the simple future is formed by adding the following endings to the stem of the verb. The endings are the same for all three conjugations:

	1st conj. (–ar)	2nd conj. (–er)	3rd conj. (–ir)
yo	cantaré	beberé	viviré
tú	cantarás	beberás	vivirás
el / ella	cantará	beberá	vivirá
nosotros/–as	cantaremos	beberemos	viviremos
vosotros/–as	cantaréis	beberéis	viviréis
ellos/ellas	cantarán	beberán	vivirán

6. Verbs

Irregular verbs

Some verbs are irregular in the future. As a general rule of thumb, the root of these verbs changes, either because they add a consonant or lose a vowel. The verbs that are irregular in the future are also irregular in the conditional.

Below, you may find the conjugations of some of the most frequent irregular future verbs which are important to remember:

decir	diré, dirás, dirá, diremos, diréis, dirán
haber	habré, habrás, habrá, habremos, habréis, habrán
hacer	haré, harás, hará, haremos, haréis, harán
poder	podré, podrás, podrá, podremos, podréis, podrán
poner	pondré, pondrás, pondrá, pondremos, pondréis, pondrán
querer	querré, querrás, querrá, querremos, querréis, querrán
saber	sabré, sabrás, sabrá, sabremos, sabréis, sabrán
salir	saldré, saldrás, saldrá, saldremos, saldréis, saldrán
tener	tendré, tendrás, tendrá, tendremos, tendréis, tendrán
valer	valdré, valdrás, valdrá, valdremos, valdréis, valdrán
venir	vendré, vendrás, vendrá, vendremos, vendréis, vendrán

Use of the simple future

The simple future is mainly used to talk about future actions and to tell us what will happen. This is why the simple future is usually used with time expressions such as those listed below:

- *luego, más tarde, pronto, mañana...* *(later, much later, soon, tomorrow)*

  Lávate las manos. Pronto comeremos. *(Wash your hands. We will be eating soon.)*

- *el próximo mes / año...* *(next month / year)*

  El próximo mes de junio se publicarán las actas. *(The minutes will be published next June.)*

- *dentro de* + time expression

  Dentro de tres meses estaremos en Roma. *(We will be in Rome in three months.)*

The simple future has other uses:

● It is used to express likelihood or supposition in the future as well as the present:

Supongo que habrá tiempo para todo. *(I guess there will be enough time for everything.)*
Seguramente saldrán a las cinco. *(They will certainly be out at five.)*
No sé que estará haciendo la niña en estos momentos. *(I don't know what the girl is doing right now.)*

● It can also be used, in an imperative sense, to express an obligation or command:

Ahora mismo irás a casa y recogerás las cosas. *(You will go home right now and get your things.)*

6.4.b. The future perfect (*futuro perfecto*)

The future perfect is used to talk about an action that will have been completed at the time we are talking about:

Cuando tú empieces tus vacaciones, nosotros ya habremos acabado las nuestras. *(When you start your vacation, we would have finished ours.)*

Conjugation

The future perfect is a compound tense formed by the future of the auxiliary verb *haber* followed by the past participle:

	1st conj. (–ar)	2nd conj. (–er)	3rd conj. (–ir)
yo	habré cantado	habré bebido	habré vivido
tú	habrás cantado	habrás bebido	habrás vivido
el / ella	habrá cantado	habrá bebido	habrá vivido
nosotros/–as	habremos cantado	habremos bebido	habremos vivido
vosotros/–as	habréis cantado	habréis bebido	habréis vivido
ellos/ellas	habrán cantado	habrán bebido	habrán vivido

The only irregularities that exist in the formation of this tense concern the past participle. Some verbs have irregular past participles, as explained in section 6.7.b. of this chapter.

VRB

Use of the future perfect

This tense compares a future action with another future action, or with a specific moment in the future. The action expressed by the future perfect will have already taken place or been completed by the time the other action or moment occurs:

> Cuando vuelvas, yo ya habré recogido todo y podremos irnos enseguida. *(When you return, I will have straightened up everything and we can leave right away.)*
> El próximo fin de semana ya habré arreglado el jardín. *(I will have the garden ready by next weekend.)*

6.5. The present conditional (*condicional simple*)

The conditional has a number of uses. It is mainly used to talk about future actions or things that are likely to happen in the present, as well as to express wishes or suggestions:

> Estas vacaciones me gustaría ir de viaje a Amberes. *(This vacation, I would like to travel to Antwerp.)*
> Juan querría tomar chocolate para merendar. *(Juan would like chocolate for his snack.)*
> Deberías estudiar más si quieres aprobar el examen. *(You should study more, if you want to pass the test.)*

6.5.a. Conjugation

Regular verbs

In Spanish, the conditional is formed by adding the following endings to the stem of the verb. The endings are the same for all three conjugations:

	1st conj. (–ar)	2nd conj. (–er)	3rd conj. (–ir)
yo	cantaría	bebería	viviría
tú	cantarías	beberías	vivirías
el / ella	cantaría	bebería	viviría
nosotros/–as	cantaríamos	beberíamos	viviríamos
vosotros/–as	cantaríais	beberíais	viviríais
ellos/ellas	cantarían	beberían	vivirían

Irregular verbs

Some verbs are irregular in the conditional. The root of these verbs changes, either because they add a consonant or lose a vowel. The verbs that are irregular in the conditional are also irregular in the future.

The following are the conjugations of the main irregular conditional verbs:

decir	diría, dirías, diría, diríamos, diríais, dirían
haber	habría, habrías, habría, habríamos, habríais, habrían
hacer	haría, harías, haría, haríamos, haríais, harían
poder	podría, podrías, podría, podríamos, podríais, podrían
poner	pondría, pondrías, pondría, pondríamos, pondríais, pondrían
querer	querría, querrías, querría, querríamos, querríais, querrían
saber	sabría, sabrías, sabría, sabríamos, sabríais, sabrían
salir	saldría, saldrías, saldría, saldríamos, saldrían, saldrían
tener	tendría, tendrías, tendría, tendríamos, tendríais, tendrían
valer	valdría, valdrías, valdría, valdríamos, valdríais, valdrían
venir	vendría, vendrías, vendría, vendríamos, vendríais, vendrían

6.5.b. Use of the present conditional

VRB

The conditional can be used in independent clauses and subordinate clauses.

Use in independent clauses

When the conditional is used independently, it has two basic meanings.

1. Firstly, it expresses possible situations that are dependent on a condition:

Si me tocara la lotería, dejaría de trabajar. *(If I won the lottery, I would quit my job.)*

It is also used to express wishes, whether they are possible or cannot be fulfilled:

Me encantaría comprarme una casa más grande. *(I would love to buy myself a bigger house.)*

2. Secondly, the tense is used as a polite way of:

- Giving advice or orders, or making suggestions:

6. Verbs

Deberías hacer los deberes cada día y no dejarlos todos para el viernes. *(You should do your homework everyday, instead of postponing it all until Friday.)*
¿**Podríamos** cambiar de tema, por favor? *(Could we please change the subject?)*
Yo de ti, lo **dejaría** tal como está. *(If I were you, I would leave it just like its is.)*

● Making a request:

¿Me **podrías** dejar tu cámara de fotos estas vacaciones? *(Could I borrow your camera for this vacation?)*

● Apologizing for not being able to do something, usually a favor:

Me **gustaría** ayudarte, pero es que tengo prisa. *(I would like to help you, but I'm in a hurry.)*

Use in subordinate clauses

The conditional can also be used in subordinate clauses to describe a past event. When the verb in the main clause is in the past, the conditional in the subordinate clause expresses an action that happened after the event in the main clause:

Me prometiste que **llegarías** antes de las ocho. *(You promised you would be here by eight.)*
Nos aseguraron que **haría** buen tiempo. *(They assured us there would be good weather.)*

6.6. The imperative (*imperativo*)

The imperative is used to give orders or commands:

Por favor, **abre** la puerta. *(Open the door, please.)*
Recordad que a las seis cierran la biblioteca. *(Remember, the library closes at six.)*

6.6.a. Conjugation

The imperative is only conjugated in the second-person singular and plural. The present subjunctive is used for the polite forms *usted* and *ustedes*. However, we will not be dealing with this aspect in this grammar as the subjunctive is one of the most complex aspects of Spanish.

Regular verbs

The imperative of regular verbs in Spanish is formed by adding the endings featured in the table below:

1st conj. (–ar)	2nd conj. (–er)	3rd conj. (–ir)
cant – a (tú)	beb – e (tú)	viv – e (tú)
cant – ad (vosotros / vosotras)	beb – ed (vosotros / vosotras)	viv – id (vosotros / vosotras)

Irregular verbs

Most verbs that form the imperative in Spanish are regular. However, there are some irregular verbs, and in most cases these irregular forms are the same as those in the present indicative.

The main irregularities in the formation of the imperative are as follows:

Radical changes

The root of the verb ends in the vowel *e* / *o*, which changes to another vowel or a diphthong in the second-person singular. The verbs with this type of irregularity are the same ones that change vowels in the present.

e ⇒ ie	**querer** *(to love / to want)*: quiere, quered *Other vebs:* *1st conj.:* acertar, cerrar, pensar, empezar, atravesar, despertar, merendar, regar, sentar, sentir, gobernar, temblar, *etc.* *2nd conj.:* entender, perder, tener, encender, entender, etc.
e ⇒ i	**pedir** *(to ask for)*: pide, pedid *Other vebs:* *3rd conj.:* conseguir, corregir, despedir, elegir, medir, repetir, seguir, perseguir, servir, reír, vestir, *etc.*
o ⇒ ue	**poder** *(can / may)*: puede, poded *Other vebs:* *1st conj.:* contar, soltar, encontrar, sonar, costar, recordar, volar, etc. *2nd conj.:* morder, volver, mover, *etc.* *3rd conj.:* dormir

VRB

6. Verbs

Consonant changes in verbs ending in –uir

The verbs ending in *–uir*, change *–ui–* to *–uy–* in the first-person plural. These verbs have the same irregularity in some persons of the present indicative.

> **ui ⇒ uy**   **huir** *(to flee / to escape):* huye, huid
> *Other vebs:*
> incluir, sustituir, construir, destruir, reconstruir, influir, distribuir, *etc.*

One-syllable imperatives in the second-person singular

Some frequently used verbs are irregular in the second-person singular of the imperative. These forms are always monosyllabic:

verb	2nd singular
dar	da
decir	di
hacer	haz
ir	ve
poner	pon
salir	sal
ser	sé
tener	ten
venir	ven

6.6.b. Use of the imperative

Value of the imperative

The imperative basically expresses orders or commands:

> ¡Cállate de una vez! *(Shut up once and for all!)*
> Busca las gafas ahora mismo. *(Go get your glasses right now.)*

It is also used to make requests, extend invitations, or give advice.

Abre la ventana, por favor. *(Open the window, please.)*
Coged un trozo de tarta, por favor. *(Please, take a piece of cake.)*
Cuídate más o al final tendrás un susto. *(Take better care of yourself or you'll have a fright.)*

In these cases, the more polite conditional tense can also be used.

Imperatives in negative sentences

It is important to know that in Spanish you never use the imperative in negative sentences. For example, it is incorrect to say **no fumad*. In negative sentences, the present subjunctive is used instead of the imperative:

Affirmative sentence	Imperative:	Habla. *(Talk.)*
Negative sentence	Present subjunctive:	No hables. *(Don't talk.)*

Imperatives with personal pronouns

In Spanish, unstressed personal pronouns always precede the verb. In the imperative, these pronouns always follow the verb:

Siéntate y bébete todo el café. *(Sit down and drink all your coffee.)*
Escúchame. *(Listen to me.)*
Coge la chaqueta y póntela. *(Get your jacket and put it on.)*

VRB

6.7. Non-finite verb forms

The non-finite verb forms are not inflected to indicate a change in person, number or tense except in certain uses of the past participles.

The non-finite verb forms in the three conjugations are:

	1st conj.	2nd conj.	3rd conj.
Infinitive	cant – ar	beb – er	viv – ir
Participle	cant – ado/a/os/as	beb – ido/a/os/as	viv – ido/a/os/as
Gerund	cant – ando	beb – iendo	viv – iendo

6.7.a. The infinitive

The infinitive is a non-finite verb form. This means that it expresses the action of the verb. However, unlike the conjugated verb forms, it does not express person, number or tense. The infinitive allows us to determine which conjugation group the verb belongs to, and it is the verb form that appears as a headword in dictionaries.

Use

The infinitive in a sentence can act as a noun and verb. It is also used in many everyday constructions in Spanish.

Use as noun and verb

Just like the other non-finite forms, the infinitive has certain characteristics that it shares with other groups of words. For instance, the infinitive can be used as a singular masculine noun and performs the syntactical functions of a noun:

> Fumar perjudica gravemente la salud. *(Smoking is severely detrimental to your health.)*
> Leer me divierte. *(I enjoy reading.)*
> Nadar es un deporte muy sano. *(Swimming is a very healthy exercise.)*
> Lo que necesita es empezar. *(What she needs is to start.)*
> Querer es poder. *(Where there is a will, there is a way.)*

Although it performs the syntactical function of a noun, in some cases it still acts as a verb and takes the corresponding objects:

> Quieren empezar una nueva vida lejos de aquí. *(They want to start a new life far away from here.)*

As it is a verb, it has a subject although, as a rule, the subject is not explicit. The subject of the infinitive is often the same as the subject of the conjugated verb.

Constructions with an infinitive

The infinitive is often used in many set constructions with their own meaning. These constructions are very common and are usually preceded by a preposition. The two most frequent ones are listed below:

- *al* + **infinitive**: has a tense value and introduces an action that takes place at the same time as another:

Al empezar el acto, todos cantaron el himno. *(They all sang the anthem when the ceremony began.)*

● *por* + **infinitive** indicates that an action that should have been done has still not been done:

Este asunto está todavía por resolver. *(This question is still to be solved.)*

The infinitive can also be used in many verb phrases, such as:

verb phrase	example
acabar de + *infinitive*	Han acabado de comer. *(They have finished lunch.)*
ir a + *infinitive*	Iré a comprar con mis amigas. *(I'll go shopping with my friends.)*
parar de + *infinitive*	¡Para ya de gritar! *(Stop shouting right now!)*
ponerse a + *infinitive*	Se puso a llover. *(It began to rain.)*
deber + *infinitive*	Deben desalojar la sala. *(You must clear the court.)*
deber (de) + *infinitive*	Deben de haber salido, no contestan. *(They must have gone out. They don't answer.)*
haber de + *infinitive*	He de salir ahora mismo. *(I must go out right away.)*
tener que + *infinitive*	Tenía que estudiar. *(She had to study.)*

VRB

6.7.b. The past participle

The past participle is a non-finite verb form. It expresses the action of the verb, but does not express number or person. The past participle is the non-finite verb form that is similar to an adjective. This means that, like many adjectives, it is inflected according to gender and number.

Formation

The past participle of regular verbs is formed by adding *–ado / –ido* to the root:

6. Verbs

1st conj. (–ar)	2nd conj. (–er)	3rd conj. (–ir)
cant – ado (sung)	beb – ido (drunk)	viv – ido (lived)

The participle is the only non-finite form that is inflected according to gender and number:

	Verb *cantar*	Verb *beber*	Verb *vivir*
masculine singular	cantado	bebido	vivido
feminine singular	cantada	bebida	vivida
masculine plural	cantados	bebidos	vividos
feminine plural	cantadas	bebidas	vividas

Irregular past participles

The past participles of most Spanish verbs are regular. However, some verbs have irregular past participles. The main irregular past participles are:

decir	dicho	*said*
hacer	hecho	*done*
abrir	abierto	*opened*
cubrir	cubierto	*covered*
descubrir	descubierto	*discovered*
describir	descrito	*described*
devolver	devuelto	*returned*
disponer	dispuesto	*readied*
disolver	disuelto	*dissolved*
envolver	envuelto	*wrapped*
escribir	escrito	*written*
morir	muerto	*died*
poner	puesto	*put*
resolver	resuelto	*solved*

romper	roto	*broken*
satisfacer	satisfecho	*satisfied*
ver	visto	*seen*
volver	vuelto	*returned*

In some cases, the irregular form is only used as an adjective, and the regular past participle is used in the compound tenses. This is the case with:

freír	*Irregular adjective:* frito.
	Ex.: un huevo frito *(a fried egg)*
	Regular participle: freído.
	Ex.: He freído un huevo. *(I have fried an egg.)*
imprimir	*Irregular adjective:* impreso.
	Ex.: un libro impreso *(a printed book)*
	Regular participle: imprimido.
	Ex.: He imprimido el libro. *(I have printed the book.)*
limpiar	*Irregular adjective:* limpio.
	Ex.: Las botas están limpias *(The boots are clean.)*
	Regular participle: limpiado.
	Ex.: He limpiado las botas. *(I have cleaned the boots.)*
soltar	*Irregular adjective:* suelto.
	Ex.: He dejado el perro suelto. *(I have left the dog loose.)*
	Regular participle: soltado.
	Ex.: He soltado al perro. *(I have left the dog off his leash.)*
despertar	*Irregular adjective:* despierto.
	Ex.: Está despierto. *(He is awake.)*
	Regular participle: despertado.
	Ex.:: He despertado a Juan. *(I have awaken Juan.)*

VRB

Use

The past participle has two distinct uses: when it is part of a compound tense and when it functions as an adjective. The past participle is also used in certain set constructions.

6. Verbs

The past participle in compound tenses

The past participle is used together with the auxiliary verb *haber* to form all the compound tenses of the verb. In this case, the past participle does not vary in gender or number, and the masculine singular form is always used:

Javier había cantado. *(Javier had sung.)*
Luisa ha cantado. *(Lusia has sung.)*
Ellos han cantado. *(They have sung.)*
Sus amigas ya habían cantado. *(Her friends had already sung.)*

In compound tenses, no words can be placed between the verb *haber* and the past participle.

The past participle used as an adjective

The past participle can also be used as an adjective. In these cases, it agrees with the noun it modifies just like any other adjective:

Javier estaba herido. *(Javier was injured.)*
Luisa parecía simpática. *(Luisa seemed nice.)*
Ellos estaban muertos. *(They were dead.)*
Sus amigas parecían cansadas. *(Her friends looked tired.)*

As an adjective, it can modify a noun:

Las chicas, cansadas de estudiar, se fueron la playa. *(The girls, tired after studying, went to the beach.)*

However, it is often used attributively with the verb *estar:*

La piscina está construida con hormigón. *(The pool was built with concrete.)*

Constructions with a past participle

The past participle is used in two different types of constructions. It is used to form the passive:

Fueron elegidos tras segunda votación. *(They were elected after a second round of votes.)*

It is used to form some verb phrases with verbs such as *ir, venir, ser, quedar, dejar, llevar,* etc.:

Luisa seguía cansada después de la siesta. *(Luisa was still tired after her nap.)*
Lleva casada ocho años. *(She's been married eight years.)*

6.7.c. The gerund

The gerund is also a non-finite verb form and, as such, it does not express time, number or person. It shares characteristics with the adverb.

Formation

The gerund is formed by adding *–ando* / *–iendo* to the root of the verb.

1st conj. *(–ar)*	2nd conj. *(–er)*	3rd conj. *(–ir)*
cant – ando *(singing)*	beb – iendo *(drinking)*	viv – iendo *(living)*

Use

The gerund performs the following functions:

- as a verb, as part of a verb phrase:

  Llevo andando tres horas.
  (I have been walking for three hours.)

- as an adverb, introducing the object of a verb:

  Lo vi saliendo del metro.
  (I saw him walking out from the subway.)

VRB

However, unlike other languages, such as English, the gerund can never accompany a noun object. This means it is incorrect to say *el hombre lle-vando un abrigo negro (the man wearing a black coat)*. In these cases, the verb is conjugated in the relevant person as part of a relative clause: *el hombre que lleva un abrigo negro (the man who wears a black coat.)*

The gerund expresses two fundamental values: duration and simultaneous action.

- When the gerund indicates duration, it refers to an action that is happening at the time of speaking or has been going on for a period of time. This meaning is often expressed using the construction *estar* + gerund:

  Estamos buscando piso. *(We are looking for an apartment.)*
  Están viendo una película de miedo. *(They are watching a terror movie.)*

6. Verbs

● The gerund can also be used to describe an action that is happening at the same time as another:

Me gusta leer el periódico tomando un café. *(I like to read newspapers while I am drinking coffee.)*

Acostumbro a comer pizza viendo la televisión. *(I have the habit to eat some pizza watching TV.)*

The gerund can also be used in many verb phrases, including:

verb phrase	example
seguir + *gerund*	Seguían haciendo quinielas. *(They continued to play the sports lottery.)*
llevar + *gerund*	Llevan toda la mañana cantando. *(They've been singing all morning.)*
ir + *gerund*	Iban decidiendo la ruta sobre la marcha. *(They were deciding their route as they went.)*

6.8. Verb phrases

Verb phrases are constructions formed by a verb conjugated in one of the tenses, followed by an infinitive, gerund or participle. A preposition can sometimes be placed between the two verbs.

Verb phrases can have a specific meaning that does not reflect the literal meaning of their components. In these constructions, the non-finite verb form (infinitive, gerund or participle) provide the lexical meaning, while the conjugated form acts as an auxiliary that lets us know the person, number, tense and aspect of the action.

Examples:

acaba de salir *(He just went out.)*	The second verb salir *provides the meaning, whereas the conjugated verb* acaba *indicates that the action finished recently.*
está cantando *(She is singing.)*	The second verb cantar *provides the meaning, whereas the conjugated verb* está *indicates that the action is ongoing.*

6.9. Special uses of some verbs

There are some verbs in Spanish that pose particular difficulties for learners. This section deals with the main ones.

6.9.a. *Ser / Estar*

Ser and *estar* are two of the most widely used verbs in Spanish. They are one of the most difficult aspects of Spanish for learners to master and among the most common causes of mistakes. The main problem comes from the fact that Spanish has two verbs for *to be*, whereas other languages, such as English, only have one. This means that it is not always easy to decide which one to use.

The specific uses of each verb are explained below.

Basic meaning

Ser is a verb used to define people and objects. Its basic meaning is to indicate the equivalence between the subject and the predicate. It is used as follows:

- To introduce inherent or permanent characteristics of people and objects:

  Roberto es alto. *(Robert is tall.)*
  Juan es amable. *(Juan is nice.)*
  Tu blusa es un diseño italiano. *(Your blouse is an Italian design.)*
  La casa es de madera. *(The house is made of wood.)*

- To classify the subject as belonging to a type or group (usually with an adjective).

  El perro es un mamífero. *(Dogs are mammals.)*
  Estas galletas son de canela. *(These are cinnamon cookies.)*

  It also specifies a job, nationality, origin or possession:

  Alfredo es arquitecto. *(Alfredo is an architect.)*
  Carlos es médico. *(Carlos is a doctor.)*
  Irene es francesa. *(Irene is French.)*
  Este ordenador es mío. *(This PC is mine.)*

Estar is used to express location or position; that is, to locate an object in space or in a phase of a process. It is used as follows:

VRB

6. Verbs

- To specify the location of an object whether temporary or permanent:

  La casa está al este de la ciudad. *(The house is east of the city.)*
  La panadería está junto a la estación. *(The bakery is beside the station.)*

- To describe temporary or transitory characteristics of a person or object (generally with an adjective):

  El abuelo está cansado. *(Grandfather is tired.)*
  El vino está pasado. *(The wine is sour.)*
  Para vacaciones, el coche estaba averiado. *(For vacation, the car was broken.)*

- To indicate whether a person or entity are in the process of doing something:

  Luis está en el primer año de universidad. *(Luis is a freshman in college.)*

Main contrasts

Due to their basic differences in meaning, *ser* and *estar* have their own distinct uses. The two main differences are listed below:

Ser is used to describe the inherent or permanent characteristics of objects or people, whereas *estar* is used to describe characteristics that can change:

  Mi hija es muy amable. *(My daughter is very nice.)* [This is a trait of her personality.]
  Mi hija hoy está muy amable. *(My daughter is very nice today.)* [She does not always behave in this way.]
  Su casa es nueva. *(His house is new.)* [It has just been built.]
  Su casa está nueva. *(His house is new.)* [It is old but well maintained.]
  Laura es nerviosa. *(Laura is nervous.)* [This is a trait of her personality.]
  Laura está nerviosa. *(Laura feels nervous.)* [Due to something that has happened.]

Estar is used to specify the location of an object. However, if we are referring to an event or to the place where an event will take place, and the date and time, we use *ser*:

  El concierto será en el auditorio. *(The concert will be in the auditorium.)*
  ¿Dónde es la lectura de poemas? *(Where is the public reading of poems?)*
  La reunión es a las doce del mediodía. *(The meeting is at midday.)*

Ser and *estar* with a past participle

Ser and *estar* can be used with a past participle. In these cases, their meaning is different:

- *Ser* + past participle is a passive construction. The passive voice focuses on the person or thing affected by an action or process. The passive voice can also be changed into the active voice, without this affecting its meaning:

Las casas fueron destruidas por el terremoto. *(The houses were destroyed by the earthquake.)* [This is the same as saying: El terremoto destruyó las casas. *(The earthquake destroyed the houses.)*]

- *Estar* + past participle focuses on the result of the action or process:

Las casas estaban destruidas. *(The houses were destroyed.)*

6.9.b. *Haber / estar*

In one of it uses, *estar* is used to describe the location of places or objects:

Madrid está en el centro de España. *(Madrid is in central Spain.)*
La goma de borrar está en el cajón. *(The eraser is in the drawer.)*

This can lead to some confusion with *haber* when it is used as the main verb (not as an auxiliary verb in compound tenses), which also describes the position of objects in a place:

Hay una goma de borrar en el cajón. *(There is an eraser in the drawer.)*

VRB

This confusion is particularly common among the speakers of other languages, such as English, who do not use two different verbs in these cases.

The main difference between the two verbs is as follows:

- *Haber* is used to introduce a new element to the discourse. Its meaning combines the notion that 'an object exists / there is an object' with the notion that 'this object is located in the place indicated'. For example, we can only use the following sentence if the stone has not been mentioned previously.

En medio del camino había una piedra. *(There was a stone in the middle of the way.)*

Given that *haber* introduces new objects into the discourse, it is always constructed with the indefinite article or without an article. It can never be constructed with the definite article or a possessive.

Hay un coche aparcado en la esquina. *(There is a parked car in the corner.)* [But not: *hay el coche aparcado en la esquina, or *hay nuestro coche aparcado en la esquina.]

6. Verbs

- *Estar* is used to indicate the location of an object or entity, when its existence is known or has been mentioned previously in the discourse:

Vi una piedra. La piedra estaba en medio del camino. *(I saw a stone. It was in the middle of the way.)*

For this reason *estar* can be used with the definite article and the possessive:

El coche está aparcado en la esquina. *(The car is parked in the corner.)*
Nuestro coche está aparcado en la esquina. *(Our car is parked in the corner.)*

6.9.c. *Saber / conocer / poder*

Spanish has three verbs related to knowledge that are close in meaning: *saber*, *conocer* and *poder*. Two of these—*saber* and *conocer*—translate into English as *to know* meaning that they can cause confusion among learners.

The main uses of these three verbs are as follows.

Basic meaning

The verb *saber* has two main uses:

- It is used to talk about skills, abilities and things people know how to do:

Sólo conozco a una persona que sabe hablar más idiomas que tú. *(I only know one person that speaks more languages than you.)*
Sé inglés, ruso y chino, pero no sé francés. *(I know English, Russian, Chinese, but I can't speak French.)*
Ya sé ir en bicicleta; ahora quiero aprender a patinar. *(I already know how to ride a bicycle. Now, I want to learn to skate.)*
No sabemos nadar, ni tocar el piano, ni dibujar, ni hacer nada especial. *(We don't know how to swim, or to play the piano, or how to draw, or doing anything special.)*

- It is used to relay information:

¿Sabes que Julia ha abandonado los estudios? *(Did you know that Julia quit school?)*
No sabía que estabas enfermo. *(I didn't know you were ill.)*

In general, it implies that the speaker has learned the information and not just heard about it:

Sé la lista de todos los elementos químicos. *(I know the list of all the chemical elements.)*
Todos sabemos que esto es difícil. *(We all know this is difficult.)*

The verb *conocer* indicates that the speaker has heard about something and also has experience or knowledge of it:

Conozco a muchos extranjeros. *(I know many foreigners.)*
Conozco todos los rincones de Barcelona. *(I know every corner in Barcelona.)*

The verb *poder* is used to talk about the skill or ability to do something, and is expressed in English by the modal verbs *can* and *to be able to*:

Nadie puede correr tanto como tú. *(No one can run as fast as you.)*
Yo sé hablar italiano, pero no puedo hablar porque estoy afónico. *(I know Italian, but I cannot speak because I have lost my voice.)*
Este cohete puede ir a la Luna y volver en pocos días. *(This rocket can fly to the Moon and back in a few days.)*

Main contrasts

In order to use these verbs correctly, it is important to bear in mind the differences between *saber* and *poder*, and *saber* and *conocer*:

- *Saber* is used for skills that imply knowledge or learning (*to play the piano, to cook, to speak languages*, etc.). In this case, *saber* is translated by the modal verbs *can* and *to be able to*. *Poder* is used to talk about somebody's ability or potential to do something. It is also translated by the modal verbs *can* and *to be able to*:

Sé dibujar caballos. *(I know how to draw horses.)*
Puedo dibujar un caballo. *(I can draw a horse.)* [It means 'I've got pencil, paper, have enough time, etc.'].

- *Saber* means the speaker has acquired information. It refers to knowledge. *Conocer* means the speaker has had experience of something. It emphasises previous experience. Both are translated by the verb *to know*:

Conozco esta teoría. *(I'm familiar with that theory.)* (I know it exists. I have heard of it.)
Sé esta teoría. *(I know that theory.)* [I have learned it. I can explain it.]

- *Conocer* can be applied to people and places.

Conozco a Juan. *(I know Juan.)* [But not *sé a Juan.]
Conozco México. *(I know Mexico.)* [But not *sé México.]

VRB

6.9.d. *Gustar* and other similar verbs

Other Spanish verbs, such as *gustar*, are constructed in different ways that can be confusing to speakers of other languages, such as English.

The verb *gustar* does not follow the normal subject + verb + object pattern of most verbs in Spanish.

The thing the person likes becomes the subject of the sentence. It is usually placed after the verb and agrees in person and number with the verb.

> Me gusta el chocolate. *(I like chocolate.)*
> Me gustan las galletas. *(I like cookies.)*

Gustar is mainly used to refer to objects, not people, so it is mostly used in the third person (singular or plural, depending on whether the subject is singular or plural).

- The person who is doing the liking is the indirect object of the sentence. The corresponding object pronoun is placed before the verb:

> Me gusta la fruta. *(I like fruit.)*
> Te gusta la fruta. *(You like fruit.)*
> Le gusta la fruta. *(He likes fruit.)*

Sometimes the indirect object is preceded by the preposition *a*:

> A Francisco le gusta el cine cómico. *(Francisco likes comedy movies.)*
> A mí no me gusta pasear. *(I don't like going out for walks.)*

Other verbs that are constructed in the same way as *gustar* are:

- Other verbs expressing liking and taste: *encantar, entusiasmar, fascinar, importar, molestar*, etc.:

> Me encantan los parques de atracciones. *(I love amusement parks.)*
> A mi madre le molesta la música demasiado alta. *(My mother dislikes music too loud.)*

- Some verbs that have a different meaning. The most important are *sorprender, pasar* (when it means *to happen*), *doler*:

> Me sorprendió tu actitud. *(I was surprised by your attitude.)*
> A Sandra le pasa algo. *(Something happens to Sandra.)*
> ¿Todavía te duele la cabeza? *(Do you still have a headache?)*

7. Adverbs

Adverbs are a class of words or phrases that are mainly used to modify or qualify a verb, indicating the circumstances—time, place, manner, etc.—in which the action is taking place:

Tu carta nos llegó ayer. *(Your letter arrived yesterday.)*
Camina despacio. *(She walks slowly.)*

Adverbs are always invariable and never inflected.

Many adverbs are formed from adjectives by adding the suffix –*mente*, in a similar way to English, which adds the suffix –*ly* to an adjective.

7.1. Types of adverbs

Adverbs can be classified into the following groups:

Time	hoy, mañana, mientras, entonces, siempre, nunca, recientemente, aún, ya, cuando, *etc.*
Manner	así, como, bien, mejor, *etc.* and most adverbs ending in –mente
Place	aquí, allí, allá, lejos, cerca, encima, debajo, abajo, *etc.*
Quantity or degree	cuanto, mucho, poco, nada, casi, bastante, demasiado, *etc.*
Affirmation	sí, cierto, también, efectivamente, *etc.*
Negation	no, tampoco, *etc.*
Probability or doubt	quizá (s), acaso, igual, posiblemente, probablemente, seguramente, *etc.*

ADV

7.1.a. Adverbs of time

Adverbs of time tell us when an action happened and usually answer the question *¿cuándo? (when?)*:

7. Adverbs

Lo tenía que acabar ayer, pero lo acabaré mañana. *(I should have finished it yesterday, but I'll finish it tomorrow.)*

They sometimes indicate how often something happens:

El concurso se convoca anualmente. *(The competition is held annually.)*

The most common adverbs of time are:

ayer, hoy, mañana	Son poesías de ayer y hoy, que no pasan con el tiempo. *(They are poems of yesterday and today, that don't go out of date.)*
	Ya han dicho el tiempo de mañana. *(They have already said what the weather will be like tomorrow.)*
	He estado corriendo toda la mañana y ahora estoy cansado. *(I've been rushing around all morning and now I'm tired.)*
antes, ahora, luego, después	Quiero llegar antes de que anochezca. *(I want to arrive before it gets dark.)*
	Pásate luego y lo hablamos. *(Drop by later and we'll talk about it.)*
	¿Por qué tenemos sueño después de comer? *(Why do we feel sleepy after we've eaten?)*
tarde, temprano, pronto	Hay gente que siempre llega tarde. *(There are some people who always arrive late.)*
	Odio levantarme temprano. *(I hate getting up early.)*
	Es tan pronto que las tiendas están cerradas. *(It's so early that the shops are closed.)*
ya, aún, todavía	¿Ya saben lo que quieren para comer o todavía no? *(Do you know what you want to eat yet or not?)*
	Aún no han llegado, pero estarán al caer. *(They're still not here, but they won't be long.)*
enseguida	Te traigo los documentos enseguida. *(I'll bring you the documents right away.)*
entonces	Entonces no vivía nadie en esta zona. *(Nobody lived in this area then.)*

	Siempre tomo un café a media mañana. *(I always have a mid-morning coffee.)*
siempre, nunca, jamás	Los exploradores nunca regresaron de aquella expedición. *(The explorers never came back from that expedition)*
	No lo hubiera dicho jamás. *(I would never have said it.)*

Some special uses

Some adverbs of time pose particular problems for learners of Spanish. Some of the special uses that you should know about are listed below.

Luego / después

These adverbs are very close in meaning: they refer to something that happened at a later time or subsequently. *Después* is usually accompanied by the preposition *de* and followed by an object:

Llegamos a casa después de las 6 de la tarde. *(We arrived home after 6 pm.)*
Lo entendí después de tu explicación. *(I understood it after your explanation.)*

However, *luego (later, later on)* is not usually followed by the preposition *de* and followed by an object. Although the construction *luego de* exists, it is very colloquial.

Temprano / pronto

Temprano can mean:

ADV

- First thing in the morning or at night:

  Siempre me levanto temprano. *(I always get up early.)*

- Over a longer period, it refers to something that happened before the expected time:

  Este año, la fruta ha madurado temprano *(This year, the fruit has ripened early.)*

The adverb *pronto* can nearly always be used in the same way as *temprano* but it can also mean 'soon', 'shortly afterwards' or 'after a while'. In this case, it cannot be used in the same way as *temprano*:

7. Adverbs

> Pronto lo sabremos. *(Soon we'll know.)* (But not **temprano lo sabremos.*)

When it has this meaning, *pronto* can go at the beginning of the sentence.

Ya / aún *and* todavía

Aún and *todavía* are synonyms and are always interchangeable. They indicate that an action or situation is continuing at a given moment:

> Mi hermano aún / todavía sigue saliendo con esa chica. *(My brother is still going out with that girl.)*

To some extent *ya* means the opposite: it indicates that the action or situation mentioned has finished. In other words, it assumes that the action used to take place but does not anymore:

> Mi hermano ya no sale con esa chica. *(My brother doesn't go out with that girl anymore.)* (It implies that he used to go out with her.)

It can also be used to express the certainty that what is being mentioned is going to happen. This usage is often not translated in English:

> Ya lo acabaré yo, no te preocupes. *(I'll finish it, don't worry.)*
> Ya nos veremos en la fiesta. *(See you at the party.)*

Nunca *and* jamás

Nunca and *jamás* are synonyms. They indicate that something has never happened or will never happen at any point in time:

> Nunca / jamás lo volveremos a ver. *(We'll never see him again.)*

These two adverbs are used in two different ways:

● They never take a negative sentence construction if they are placed before the verb:

> Jamás / nunca lo descubrirás. *(You'll never find out.)*

● However, when they follow the verb, a double negative sentence construction must be used:

> No lo descubrirás jamás / nunca. *(You'll never find out.)*

Both adverbs can be used together to emphasize meaning in the set phrase *nunca jamás*, which is the equivalent of saying «never ever» or «never, never» in English:

> No lo descubrirás nunca jamás. *(You'll never ever find out.)*

7.1.b. Adverbs of manner

Adverbs of manner tell us about the way something happened and usually answer the question ¿cómo? (how?):

El pianista tocaba muy bien. *(The pianist played very well.)*
Los árboles crecen despacio. *(Trees grow slowly.)*
Trepó al árbol ágilmente. *(He climbed nimbly up the tree.)*

Most adverbs of manner end in –*mente*: *hábilmente, discretamente, silenciosamente, claramente, rápidamente, voluntariamente, alegremente,* etc. There is a group of adverbs of manner that do not take the ending –*mente*: *bien, mal, así,* etc.

Adverbs ending in –*mente*

Most adverbs of manner take the suffix –*mente*:

Se incorporó al nuevo equipo paulatinamente. *(He gradually settled into the new team.)*
Entró sigilosamente para no despertar a nadie. *(He came in quietly so he wouldn't wake anybody up.)*
Buscaban desesperadamente a su hija. *(They were desperately looking for their daughter.)*

These adverbs are formed by taking the feminine singular form of the adjective and adding the ending –*mente*:

Adjective	Adverb
rápido, rápida *(rapid, quick)*	rápidamente
brusco, brusca *(sudden; brusque)*	bruscamente
lógico, lógica *(logical)*	lógicamente
supuesto, supuesta *(supposed, assumed)*	supuestamente
difícil *(difficult)*	difícilmente
especial *(special)*	especialmente
alegre *(happy, cheerful)*	alegremente
prudente *(prudent, sensible)*	prudentemente

ADV

Adverbs can also be formed from the superlative feminine singular form of the adjective: *rapidísimamente, frecuentísimamente, clarísimamente, facilísimamente*, etc.

Not all adjectives in Spanish can be transformed into adverbs of manner by adding the ending *−mente*. This is the case with adjectives of nationality, such as *francés, inglés, canadiense*, etc., as well as adjectives indicating color, such as *rojo, amarillo, negro*, etc. As a general rule of thumb, you can form adverbs with *−mente* in Spanish with the same adjectives that can be used to form adverbs ending in *−ly* in English.

There are some exceptions. For instance, most ordinal numbers do not have an adverbial form in Spanish (**segundamente, *terceramente, *cuartamente*, etc. do not exist). *Primeramente* and *últimamente* are the only two correct forms.

When two or more adverbs of manner follow one another, *−mente* is omitted from all but the last one:

> Salió de la conferencia discreta y silenciosamente. *(He left the lecture discreetly and quietly.)*
> Resuelve los ejercicios rápida y eficazmente. *(She does the exercises quickly and efficiently.)*

Adverbs of manner not formed from adjectives

Some adverbs of manner are not formed by adding the ending *−mente* and are words in their own right: *bien, mal, así, deprisa, despacio*:

> Todo el equipo ha jugado mal hoy. *(The whole team played badly today.)*
> Se encuentra muy bien después de la operación. *(He's feeling very well after the operation.)*
> No voy a consentir que se burlen así de mí. *(I won't let them make fun of me like that.)*

Some adjectives can be used in their masculine singular form to make adverbs. Many of these adverbs are only used with specific verbs.

The main adverbs formed from masculine singular adjectives are:

claro	Lo he dicho muy claro. *(I said it very clearly.)*
alto, bajo	Habla muy bajo / alto. *(He speaks very quietly / loud.)*
barato, caro, gratis	Me ha salido barato / caro / gratis. *(It turned out to be cheap / expensive / free.)*

diferente, distinto	Los dos me gustan, aunque cantan diferente / distinto. *(I like them both, although they sing differently.)*
duro	Tendremos que trabajar duro. *(We'll have to work hard.)*
estupendo, fatal, fenomenal, genial, perfecto, súper	Lo has hecho estupendo / fatal / fenomenal / genial / perfecto / súper. *(You've done it wonderfully / terribly / terrifically / brilliantly / perfectly / fantastically.)*
fácil	Esto se arregla fácil. *(This will get sorted easily.)*
lento, rápido	Camina lento / rápido. *(He walks slowly / quickly.)*

7.1.c. Adverbs of place

Adverbs of place tell us where something happened and usually answer the question ¿dónde? *(where?)*.

The most common adverbs of place are:

cerca / lejos	Busca un hotel cerca del centro de Madrid. *(She's looking for a hotel near the center of Madrid.)*
	Las navidades lejos de casa son muy tristes. *(It's sad to spend Christmas far from home.)*
arriba / abajo	Hay mejores vistas desde arriba. *(The views are better from up there.)*
	Si miras hacia abajo te marearás. *(If you look down, you'll feel dizzy.)*
encima / debajo	No pongas los pies encima de la mesa. *(Don't put your feet on the table.)*
	Dejó los zapatos debajo de la cama. *(He left his shoes under the bed.)*
delante, enfrente / detrás	No es fácil ponerse delante de las cámaras de televisión. *(It's not easy to stand in front of the television cameras.)*
	Justo enfrente de casa han abierto una nueva tienda. *(They've just opened a new store just opposite our house.)*
	Nos escondimos detrás de la mesa para darle una sorpresa. *(We hid behind the table to give her a surprise.)*

ADV

dentro / fuera	Dentro de la cárcel no hay muchas diversiones. *(There's not much fun to be had in prison.)*
	Sácalo fuera de la habitación, por favor. *(Bring him out of the room, please.)*
alrededor	Soñaba con hacer un viaje alrededor de la Luna. *(He dreamt of going on a voyage around the moon.)*
aquí – acá / ahí / allí – allá	Viven aquí mismo, muy cerca del colegio. *(They live right here, very near the school.)*
	Yo soy mexicano de acá, de este lado de la frontera. *(I'm a Mexican from round here, from this side of the border.)*
	Están construyendo una piscina nueva allí. *(They're building a new swimming pool over there.)*
	Ponte más hacia allá. *(Move further over there.)*
	Lo tienes ahí mismo, pero no puedes verlo. *(It's right there, but you can't see it.)*

Some special uses: *aquí, allí, acá* and *allá*

Spanish has three groups of adverbs to express the concept of 'here' or 'there'. They are used according to how near or far away somebody or something is from the person speaking or being spoken to:

aquí, acá	Closeness to the speaker
	Ven aquí. (Come here.)
ahí	Closeness to the addressee
	Déjalo ahí, a tu lado. (Leave it there, next to you.)
allí, allá	Distance from the speaker and addressee
	Lo vi allá a lo lejos. (I saw it over there in the distance.)

To use them correctly, it is important to bear in mind the following:

- *Aquí* is mainly used in Spain, whereas *acá* is only used in Latin American Spanish.

- *Allí* refers to a more precise location than *allá*, which is less specific:

  El libro está allí, en el tercer estante. *(The book is over there, on the third shelf.)*
  Allá se vive mejor que aquí. *(People live better there than they do here.)*

7.1.d. Adverbs of quantity or degree

This group of adverbs tells us about the different degrees of intensity of an action. Some of them can also be used as determiners or pronouns.

The most common adverbs of quantity or degree are:

demasiado,	Grita demasiado. *(He shouts too much.)*
muy,	Tengo muy buenos recuerdos de aquel viaje.
mucho,	*(I have very good memories of that trip.)*
bastante,	Come mucho. *(He eats a lot.)*
algo,	Este verano ha crecido bastante. *(He's grown*
poco,	*quite a lot this summer.)*
apenas,	El paciente ha mejorado algo. *(The patient has*
nada	*improved slightly.)*
	Habla español, pero muy poco. *(He speaks*
	Spanish, but very little.)
	Apenas se le oye. *(You can hardly hear him.)*
	Últimamente no duerme nada. *(She hasn't*
	slept at all lately.)
más,	Nunca está satisfecho; siempre quiere más.
menos	*(He's never satisfied; he always wants more.)*
	No puedes trabajar más y cobrar menos. *(You*
	can't work more and earn less.)
casi	Casi ha terminado la carrera. *(She's almost*
	finished her degree.)
tan / tanto	No vayas tan deprisa; puedes tener un
	accidente. *(Don't go so fast; you might have*
	an accident.)
	Hacía tiempo que no comía tanto. *(I haven't*
	eaten so much for ages.)

ADV

Some special uses

Apocopated forms

Tan and *muy* are the apocopated forms of *tanto* and *mucho*. They are only used in front of adjectives and adverbs:

7. Adverbs

tan alto *(so tall, so high)*
tan deprisa *(so quickly)*
muy alto *(very tall, very high)*
muy deprisa *(very fast)*

The full form is used when the adverb modifies a verb:

Corre mucho. *(He runs a lot.)*
¡Sabe tanto! *(She knows so much!)*

Comparisons

The forms *más* and *menos* are used in comparisons. They can compare adjectives, adverbs and verbs:

Es más / menos alto que tú. *(He's taller / not as tall as you.)*
Corre más / menos deprisa que tú. *(He runs more quickly / less quickly than you.)*
Habla más / menos que tú. *(He speaks more / less than you.)*

7.1.e. Adverbs of affirmation and negation

These adverbs are used to affirm or refute a statement:

Tú dices que no lo entiendes, pero yo sí lo entiendo. *(You say that you don't understand it, but I do understand it.)*

They can be used as part of a sentence, or separately like all affirmative or negative responses:

—¿Nos acompañarás mañana a la playa? *(Will you come with us to the beach tomorrow?)*
—Sí. / No. *(Yes. / No.)*

Strictly speaking, the adverbs of affirmation and negation are *sí / no* and *también / tampoco*. However, other adverbs can be used:

—¿Nos ayudarás? *(Will you help us?)*
—Ciertamente. / Efectivamente. / Jamás. *(Certainly. / Of course. / Never.)*

Some special uses: *también* and *tampoco*

También and *tampoco* are used to refer to something that happened at the same time as a preceding affirmation or negation:

Susana quiere venir y yo también. *(Susana wants to come and I do too.)*
A Teresa no le gustan las películas de terror y a mí tampoco. *(Teresa doesn't like horror movies and neither do I.)*

When *tampoco* is placed after the verb, you need to use a double negative construction. However, if it precedes the verb, you don't:

Daniel tampoco lo sabe. *(Daniel doesn't know either.)*
Daniel no lo sabe tampoco. *(Daniel doesn't know either.)*

7.1.f. Adverbs of possibility or doubt

Adverbs of possibility or doubt indicate different degrees on a scale of probability. The most common are listed below:

quizá (s)	Quizá (s) estamos equivocados. *(Maybe we're wrong.)*
tal vez	Tal vez vaya a verlo mañana. *(Perhaps he'll go and see him tomorrow.)*
posiblemente, probablemente, seguramente	Posiblemente iré a estudiar al extranjero. *(Maybe I'll go and study abroad.)*
seguro	Seguro que ganas tú. *(You're sure to win.)*

From a syntactical viewpoint, one of the difficulties posed by the use of these adverbs is that some of them require the use of the subjunctive. We will not be dealing with the subjunctive in this grammar as it corresponds to a higher level of Spanish.

ADV

7.2. Comparatives using adverbs

Adverbs are a class of word that shares some similarities with adjectives. For instance, most adverbs (all adverbs ending in –*mente* and many others that are not formed from adjectives) can be used to express comparison. Adverbs can express the same degree of comparison as adjectives: superiority, inferiority and equality.

7.2.a. Comparative of superiority

The comparative of superiority is formed by placing *más* in front of the adverb which is followed by *que*:

7. Adverbs

- *más* + adverb:

  Habla más claro, por favor. *(Speak more clearly please.)*

- *más* + adverb + *que*:

  Escribe más deprisa que el resto de niños de la clase. *(He writes more quickly than the other children in his class.)*

7.2.b. Comparative of inferiority

The comparative of inferiority is formed by placing *menos* in front of the adverb which is followed by *que*:

- *menos* + adverb:

  Ha de defender su posición menos acaloradamente. *(He must defend his position less heatedly.)*

- *menos* + adverb + *que*:

  Hemos conseguido llegar menos tarde que ayer. *(We managed to arrive earlier than yesterday.)*

7.2.c. Comparative of equality

The comparative of equality is formed with constructions such as *tan... como* and *igual de... que*:

- *tan* + adverb + *como*:

  Va tan rápido como su hermano. *(He goes as fast as his brother.)*

- *igual de* + adverb (+ *que*):

  Come igual de mal que su hermano. *(He eats just as badly as his brother.)*

7.3.   The position of the adverb in the sentence

In Spanish, the position of the adverb is quite flexible and it can go in different places in the sentence.

For example, in the sentence below, the adverb *allí* can go before the verb, immediately after the verb and at the end of the sentence:

Allí aprendí a hablar francés.
Aprendí allí a hablar francés.
Aprendí a hablar francés allí.

As you can see, Spanish differs from other languages, such as English, which has stricter rules regarding the order of the adverb in the sentence. For instance, in the above sentence in English, the adverb can only be placed at the end of the sentence: *I learnt to speak French there.*

However, although adverbs can often go in different positions in a sentence, there are some cases when they have to appear in a specific position, depending on how they are used.

- Adverbs that modify an adjective or another adverb are always placed before the adjective or adverb being modified:

  Habla muy deprisa y bastante desordenadamente. *(He speaks very quickly and rather unclearly.)*
  Es muy alto y francamente guapo. *(He's very tall and really handsome.)*

- Adverbs that modify a verb (adverbs of manner, time or place) are usually placed after the verb or the other verb objects:

  Aprendió las tablas de multiplicar deprisa. *(She learnt her times table quickly.)*
  Acabaré enseguida los deberes. *(I'll finish my homework right away.)*

- Adverbs that modify an entire sentence—indicating the speaker's assessment of a situation, opinion and attitude, or the likelihood of something happening—are usually placed at the beginning of the sentence, or elsewhere in the sentence, separated by commas:

  Francamente, no te entiendo. *(Frankly, I don't understand you.)*
  El presidente, muy hábilmente, evitó hablar de la crisis económica. *(Very skillfully, the president avoided talking about the economic crisis.)*
  Posiblemente esto no es cierto. *(Maybe it's not true.)*

ADV

8. Prepositions

Prepositions are words that are used to link two words or elements in a sentence. This means that they can never stand alone. In Spanish, prepositions are a closed word class. In other words, they consist of a set list of words. Therefore, no new ones can be added. These words have two basic characteristics:

- They are invariable. In other words, they are not inflected and do not take a suffix.

- They are always unstressed (with the exception of *según*).

8.1. Forms

Prepositions are a closed word class. This means, as we have said before, that no other words can be added to them. The list of prepositions in Spanish is as follows:

a	contra	en	mediante	sin
ante	de	entre	para	sobre
bajo	desde	hacia	por	tras
con	durante	hasta	según	

Some of these prepositions are commonly used in written Spanish but seldom appear in spoken Spanish, which tends to replace them with prepositional phrases. This happens with the three cases below:

In written Spanish	In spoken Spanish
ante *(in front of)*	delante de *is used instead of* ante
tras *(behind)*	detrás de *or* después de *are used instead of* tras
bajo *(below)*	debajo de *is used instead of* bajo

8.2. Values

Prepositions link two words or elements in a sentence. They can have a variety of meanings and show the relationship between the two words or elements they connect. However, there are certain prepositions that mean nothing themselves but perform a syntactical function.

Broadly speaking, there are three semantic groups of prepositions:

- Prepositions which have meaning in their own right, such as *sin* or *bajo*, which clearly show the relationship between the elements they connect. For example:

ante *(in front of something)*	Ante nosotros se alzaba la catedral. *(The cathedral towered in front of us.)*
bajo *(in a lower position or place)*	Lo vi bajo la ventana. *(I saw him below the window.)*
sin *(a lack or shortage of something)*	Regresó sin dinero. *(He came back without any money.)*
sobre *(on top of something)*	El jarrón está sobre la mesa. *(The vase is on the table.)*

- Some prepositions are more versatile and have different meanings according to their context. For example, *con*::

  instrument: Córtalo con el cuchillo. *(Cut it with the knife.)*
  contents: Llenó un vaso con agua. *(She filled the glass with water.)*
  company: Está con su abuela. *(He's with his grandma.)*

  PREP

- Some Spanish prepositions do not have a literal meaning and are only used to indicate a type of grammatical relationship. In English, we don't use preposition in these cases. For example, the preposition *a* that introduces a direct object if the direct object is a person (*vi a Manuel [I saw Manuel]*) or the preposition *de* in constructions like *calle de Morelos (Morelos Street.)*

8.3. Main uses of prepositions in Spanish

8.3.a. *A*

The preposition *a* is one of the prepositions that has the widest variety of uses in Spanish. Its meaning often depends on context. In some cases, it has no literal meaning but highlights the grammatical function of an element.

The most common uses of *a* when it has a literal meaning are listed below:

- It expresses movement towards a particular destination, point or objective:

  Voy a Madrid todos los lunes. *(I go to Madrid on Mondays.)*
  Toda su vida se dirige a la consecución de sus objetivos. *(All his life has been geared towards achieving his aims.)*
  A primera hora van a clase de guitarra. *(They go to guitar classes first thing in the morning.)*

- It also expresses distance. In these cases, it is generally used with the verb *estar*:

  La playa está a seis kilómetros. *(The beach is six kilometers away.)*
  Está a unas dos horas en coche. *(It's about two hours away by car.)*

- It introduces expressions of time:

  La película empieza a las seis de la tarde. *(The movie begins at 6 pm.)*
  Llegarán al aeropuerto a las once. *(They'll arrive at the airport at 11 am.)*
  Han quedado en el restaurante a mediodía. *(They've arranged to meet at the restaurant at lunchtime.)*

- It indicates how old somebody is when they do something:

  A los dieciocho años te puedes sacar el carnet de conducir. *(You can take your driving test at the age of eighteen.)*
  Se graduó a los veintitrés años. *(She graduated at the age of twenty-three.)*

- It expresses how something is made or done as well as the method or instrument used:

  Sólo venden cosas hechas a mano. *(They only sell hand-made things.)*
  Fuimos a pie. *(We went on foot.)*
  Me gusta la merluza a la romana. *(I love hake in batter.)*

In two cases, the preposition *a* has no literal meaning but highlights a grammatical relationship.

- It introduces a direct object if the direct object is a person:

  Vi a María cuando salía del metro. *(I saw María when she was coming out of the subway.)*
  Voy a buscar a mis padres al médico. *(I'm going to pick up my parents from the doctor's.)*

- It introduces an indirect object:

  Le han buscado un piso a Luis. *(They've been looking for a flat for Luis.)*
  Le tengo que dar las gracias a tu hermana por haberme traído hasta aquí. *(I must thank your sister for bringing me here.)*
  A todo el mundo le gustan los piropos. *(Everybody likes compliments.)*

8.3.b. *Ante*

The preposition *ante* indicates that something is in front of somebody or something. It is equivalent to *frente a* and *delante de*, which are normally used in spoken Spanish instead of *ante*:

  Se encontraba ante el museo del Prado. *(He was in front of the Prado Museum.)*
  Se manifestaron ante el Ayuntamiento. *(They demonstrated in front of city hall.)*

It is often used in a figurative sense when people are confronted with something. In this case, *frente a* and *delante de* cannot be used in its place:

  Muchos estudiantes padecen ansiedad ante los exámenes. *(A lot of students suffer from anxiety when faced with their exams.)*
  Los bomberos actuaron con arrojo ante el peligro. *(The firefighters acted bravely in the face of danger.)*
  Me inclino ante tu sabiduría. *(I bow to your wisdom.)*

8.3.c. *Bajo*

The preposition *bajo* is mainly used in more formal language. It indicates that something is under something else. It is equivalent to *debajo de*, which is used more often in spoken Spanish:

  El perro esperaba en la sombra, bajo el árbol. *(The dog was waiting in the shade, under the tree.)*
  Encontrarás las llaves de casa bajo la alfombrilla. *(You'll find the house keys under the mat.)*

PREP

It is often used figuratively and in these cases cannot be replaced with *debajo de*:

No me gusta conducir bajo la lluvia. *(I don't like driving in the rain.)*
Para los agricultores es imprescindible que las plagas estén bajo control. *(For farmers, it is essential to keep pests under control.)*
Este medicamento debe administrarse bajo control médico. *(This medicine must be taken under medical supervision.)*

8.3.d. *Con*

The preposition *con* is basically used to indicate that somebody is accompanying somebody else or to refer to the instrument used to perform an action.

- It introduces an object that indicates company:

  Pasó todo el verano con nosotros. *(He spent all summer with us.)*
  Quería compartir piso con ella. *(He wanted to share an apartment with her.)*

- It introduces the object of some verbs that indicate the relationship between two people:

  Se casó con Álvaro a los veinte años. *(She got married to Álvaro when she was twenty.)*
  Juega al ajedrez con su padre. *(She plays chess with her father.)*

- It indicates the instrument, material or method used to do something:

  Abre la puerta con la llave. *(He opens the door with the key.)*
  Ya sabe comer con cubiertos. *(He already knows how to eat with cutlery.)*
  Con perseverancia conseguirá acabar los estudios. *(He'll manage to finish his studies if he perseveres.)*
  Se defendió con todas sus fuerzas. *(He defended himself with all his might.)*

It also has other uses that are not associated with these meanings.

- It indicates the characteristics of an object or person. These are usually objects that refer to the parts that make up a whole:

  Busca un apartamento con aire acondicionado. *(He's looking for an apartment with air conditioning.)*
  Quieren un hotel con piscina. *(They want a hotel with a swimming pool.)*
  Prefiere los hombres con bigote. *(She prefers men with mustaches.)*

- It also indicates the contents of something, particularly a container:

  Dame un vaso con agua, por favor. *(Give me a glass of water, please.)*
  El vehículo circulaba con seis ocupantes. *(The vehicle was carrying six passengers.)*

8.3.e. *Contra*

The preposition *contra* mainly indicates opposition or confrontation:

El domingo juega el equipo de nuestra universidad contra el ganador del año pasado. *(On Sunday, our university team is playing against last year's winner.)*
Se convocó una manifestación contra la bajada de sueldos. *(A demonstration was called against the drop in salaries.)*
Hay un gran movimiento contra la violencia de género. *(There is a large-scale movement against gender violence.)*

It can also indicate the position of an object or person in relation to something else:

Puso la cara contra el viento. *(He turned his face to the wind.)*
El barco avanzaba contra la corriente. *(The boat moved forward against the tide.)*
Puso la mesa contra la pared. *(He put the table against the wall.)*

8.3.f. *De*

De is one of the most widely used and versatile prepositions in Spanish. Its variety of uses means that it is often necessary to look at the context to work out its meaning.

It is mainly used to introduce noun objects that indicate the following:

- Possession:

Los libros de Juan están en el despacho. *(Juan's books are in the office.)*
La melena de Sara despierta admiración. *(Sara's long hair is greatly admired.)*
Las luces del restaurante se han de cambiar. *(The lights in the restaurant need changing.)*

- The characteristics of an object or person:

Era una mujer de ojos claros, de mirada franca y de hablar sereno. *(She had pale eyes, a candid gaze and was softly spoken.)*
Los soldados eran hombres de valor. *(The soldiers were men of courage.)*

- The material something is made of:

Las sillas de madera eran muy cómodas. *(The wooden chairs were very comfortable.)*
Las luces de neón no deslumbran. *(Neon lights don't dazzle you.)*
Me gusta el queso de cabra. *(I love goat's cheese.)*

PREP

8. Prepositions

- The price of something:

  Un coche de doce mil dólares. *(A twelve-thousand-dollar car.)*

- The origin of something:

  Los aguacates de Centroamérica son muy sabrosos. *(Avocados from Central America are very tasty.)*
  La lana de Escocia es muy apreciada. *(Scottish wool is highly prized.)*

- The contents of something:

  Tomó un vaso de leche. *(He had a glass of milk.)*
  La caja de zapatos no quería guardarla. *(He didn't want to keep the shoebox.)*

- To refer to the time of day after expressions of time:

  Son las seis de la tarde. *(It's six in the evening.)*
  Aterrizaron a las diez de la mañana. *(They landed at ten in the morning.)*
  Las estrellas salen de noche. *(Stars come out at night.)*

- Somebody's age:

  Tengo un hermano de treinta años y otro de veintitrés. *(I have a brother of thirty and another of twenty-three.)*

It is important to note that, unlike the preposition *a*, *de* does not refer to how old somebody is when they do something, but to indicate the age of the person they are talking about.

De also introduces the objects of some verbs. These include:

- Objects of place that indicate origin in space or time:

  Ayer llegaron de Boston para pasar las vacaciones en España. *(They arrived from Boston yesterday to spend their vacation in Spain.)*
  La recepción está abierta de ocho de la mañana a ocho de la noche. *(The reception is open from eight in the morning until eight in the evening.)*

The construction *de … a* is commonly used to talk about the beginning and end of an action, especially to refer to periods of time:

  Trabaja en la oficina de lunes a viernes. *(He works at the office from Monday to Friday.)*
  De ocho a cuatro, tiene el celular desconectado. *(He switches off his cellphone from eight to four.)*

- Some expressions of manner:

  Es mejor trabajar cuando estás de buen humor. *(It's better to work when you're in a good mood.)*

Estaba de pie delante de la estantería. *(He was standing in front of the bookcase.)*
Al oír el timbre se levantó de golpe. *(He jumped up when he heard the bell.)*

8.3.g. *Desde*

The preposition *desde* indicates the origin or starting point of something in either time or space, or movement from a certain point or place.

- It indicates where an action originates, the point of departure:

  Vienen en coche desde San Diego. *(They're coming by car from San Diego.)*

- It indicates the starting point of an action that is continuing:

  Está buscando piso desde Navidad. *(She's been looking for an apartment since Christmas.)*

- It indicates the point or time when an action began:

  Desde aquel momento, todo en su vida cambió. *(From that moment, his life changed.)*

- It indicates a place of origin where something is done:

  Trabajar desde casa cada vez es más frecuente. *(It's increasingly common for people to work from home.)*
  Te escribo desde París. *(I'm writing you from Paris.)*

The construction *desde … hasta* is commonly used to talk about the beginning and end of an action, or the scope of such an action:

Desde las cinco hasta las siete tiene danza. *(She has her dance class from five to eight.)*
El catálogo de la editorial abarca desde Educación Infantil hasta Bachillerato. *(The publisher's catalogue covers subjects ranging from Children's Education to High-School Education.)*

PREP

8.3.h. *Durante*

The preposition *durante* is basically used to express the duration or persistence of an action in time. Its two main uses are:

- To express simultaneity. It indicates that the action of the verb is taking place during the same period of time as the action being mentioned:

8. Prepositions

> Durante las vacaciones fuimos cada día a la playa. (*During the vacation we went to the beach every day.*)
> No me gusta ver la televisión durante la cena. (*I don't like watching television during dinner.*)
> Fumar durante el embarazo puede poner en peligro la salud de la mujer y la de su bebé. (*Smoking during pregnancy can endanger the health of a woman and her baby.*)

- It can also express the duration of an action:

> Declaró durante más de seis horas. (*He took more than six hours to make a statement.*)
> Publicó un artículo sobre las actividades de un político durante su jornada.
> (*He published an article on the activities of a politician during his working day.*)

8.3.i. *En*

The preposition *en* is basically used to indicate the location or position of something in both space and time.

- It indicates the place where the action happens:

> Esta semana Mario está en Bruselas. (*This week Mario is in Brussels.*)
> Siempre estudio en mi dormitorio. (*I always study in my bedroom.*)
> Olvidó la chaqueta en el sofá. (*He left his jacket on the sofa.*)

- It indicates the time when the action happens:

> Aprendió a ir en bicicleta en verano. (*He learnt to ride a bike in summer.*)
> En enero se apuntó al gimnasio. (*He joined the gym in January.*)
> Nació en 1971. (*She was born in 1971.*)

- It is used to refer to the means of transport somebody uses:

> Siempre voy a trabajar en tren. (*I always go to work by train.*)
> Va en bicicleta a todas partes. (*He goes everywhere by bike.*)

- It indicates the time it takes to finish something:

> Tuvo resuelto el problema en cinco minutos. (*He had the problem solved in five minutes.*)
> Preparó el viaje en un par de meses. (*He prepared the trip in a couple of months.*)

8.3.j. *Entre*

The preposition *entre* indicates the position of something or somebody between two things or more. When it has this meaning:

- It indicates the physical space separating two or more things:

  Vive **entre** Madrid y Londres. *(He lives between Madrid and London.)*
  Espera **entre** las dos puertas. *(She's waiting between the two doors.)*
  Lo distinguió **entre** los árboles. *(She could make him out between the trees.)*

- It indicates an interval of time between two moments or periods:

  Los niños **entre** diez y doce años participarán en las pruebas de atletismo. *(Children aged between ten and twelve will take place in the athletics trials.)*

- It indicates a property between two possible extremes:

  Este helado es **entre** dulce y amargo. *(This ice cream is both sweet and bitter.)*
  Me siento **entre** triste y enfadado. *(I feel sad and angry at the same time.)*

It can also express an idea of cooperation or reciprocity between or among several people.

- It indicates a reciprocal action:

  Hablaron **entre** ellas sobre cómo resolver la situación. *(They spoke among themselves about how to resolve the situation.)*

- It expresses cooperation between several people:

  Entre todos lograremos triunfar. *(Between all of us, we'll manage to succeed.)*
  Al final acabaron la mudanza **entre** los tres. *(They ended up finishing the move between the three of them.)*

8.3.k. *Hacia*

The preposition *hacia* expresses both location and time:

- It indicates movement towards an object or person:

  Salieron **hacia** Tucson muy temprano. *(They left for Tucson very early.)*
  Todas las miradas se dirigieron **hacia** él. *(All eyes turned toward him.)*

- It expresses an imprecise, approximate time:

  Creo que nos conocimos **hacia** el año 1990, cuando acababa de llegar a la ciudad. *(I think we met around 1990, when I had just arrived in town.)*
  Quedamos **hacia** las seis en el cine. *(Let's meet around six at the theater.)*

PREP

8.3.l. *Hasta*

The preposition *hasta* is used to refer to destination and to the period up to a specific point in time. Basically, it has two uses.

- It indicates the end of an action or situation in space and time:

  Fueron hasta el final del pueblo a ver si la encontraban. *(They went as far as the end of the village to see if they could find her.)*
  Le esperarán despiertos hasta medianoche. *(They stayed up to wait for her until midnight.)*
  Los británicos tendrán que trabajar hasta los 66 años. *(The British will have to work until they're 66.)*

- It indicates the level something has reached:

  El agua me llegaba hasta las rodillas. *(The water came up to my knees.)*

It is also used in a number of expressions to say goodbye to somebody you are going to see in the time indicated:

  Hasta luego. *(See you later.)*
  Hasta pronto. *(See you soon.)*
  Hasta la vuelta. *(See you when I / you / we get back.)*
  Hasta mañana. *(See you tomorrow.)*
  Hasta ahora. *(See you in a minute.)*

8.3.m. *Mediante*

The preposition *mediante* expresses the means by which something is achieved. It is equivalent to 'with the help of' or 'thanks to':

  Aprende inglés mediante juegos. *(He's learning English through games.)*
  Es una batería recargable mediante energía solar. *(This battery can be recharged by solar energy.)*
  ¿Se encuentra trabajo mediante las redes sociales? *(Can you find work through social media?)*

8.3.n. *Para*

The preposition *para* has many uses in Spanish and, as a rule, its meaning can only be worked out through context. It also poses frequent problems for learners of Spanish because of the confusion that sometimes occurs between *por* and *para*.

The most common uses of *para* are:

- To indicate the objective or purpose of an action or thing:

  Estudia para aprobar los exámenes de setiembre. *(She's studying to pass her exams in September.)*
  Sigue una dieta para adelgazar. *(He's following a diet to lose weight.)*
  Ha conseguido una beca para seguir sus estudios en el extranjero. *(She's received a scholarship to continue studying abroad.)*

- To indicate the beneficiary of an action:

  Compraron el juguete para su hijo. *(They bought the toy for their son.)*
  Es un libro de español para extranjeros. *(It's a book of Spanish for foreigners.)*
  Sigue un programa de cocina para principiantes. *(He's taking a cookery course for beginners.)*

- When placed with certain verbs, nouns or adjectives, it expresses the use or purpose of something:

  Hemos comprado tela para un vestido. *(We've bought some fabric for a dress.)*
  Es bueno para la salud beber mucha agua. *(Drinking a lot of water is good for your health.)*

- It can also be used to refer to destinations:

  Saldremos mañana para Buenos Aires.
  (We will leave for Buenos Aires tomorrow.)

- It indicates a period of time in the future:

  Lo tendrán acabado para mañana. *(They'll have it finished by tomorrow.)*
  He comprado fruta para el domingo. *(I've bought some fruit for Sunday.)*

- When preceded by a proper noun or a personal pronoun, it indicates that the expression that follows is an opinion:

  Para mí, te estás equivocando. *(In my opinion, you're making a mistake.)*

PREP

8.3.ñ. *Por*

The preposition *por* has many uses in Spanish and its meaning is often contextual. It also poses frequent problems for learners of Spanish because of the confusion that sometimes arises between *por* and *para*.

The most common uses of *por* are:

8. Prepositions

● It expresses the place through which, or along which, a movement takes place:

Pasaremos por Richmond. *(We'll pass through Richmond.)*
Me encanta pasear por la playa. *(I love to walk along the beach.)*
El transporte por carretera ha aumentado en los últimos años. *(Transport by road has increased over the past few years.)*
Entra por la puerta derecha. *(Enter by the door on the right.)*
Por estas calles no pasa nadie. *(Nobody goes along these streets.)*

● It indicates the cause, motivation or reason for something in a broad sense:

Muchas personas están en paro por la crisis económica. *(Many people are unemployed because of the economic crisis.)*
Fue a vivir a Chipre por amor. *(He went to live in Cyprus because he was in love.)*
Se suspendió el partido por la lluvia. *(The game was suspended because of the rain.)*

● It indicates that something was done by somebody:

Es un libro de cuentos ilustrados por niños. *(It's a storybook illustrated by children.)*
El edificio fue diseñado por un gran arquitecto. *(The building was designed by a great architect.)*

● It indicates an approximate time, and is used particularly with dates:

Vamos a casa por Navidad. *(We're going home for Christmas.)*
Vendremos por la mañana. *(We're going to come in the morning.)*

When referring to time, it can never indicate the duration of an action. In these cases, we use the preposition *durante*:

He hablado durante más de una hora. *(I've been speaking for more than an hour.)* Not *por una hora.

● It indicates the means by which something is achieved:

Hablé por teléfono con Jenny. *(I spoke to Jenny by phone.)*
Paga los recibos por el banco. *(He pays his bills through the bank.)*

● It introduces the second number in multiplications:

Cinco por dos es igual diez. *(Five times two is ten.)*

8.3.o. *Según*

The preposition *según* is mainly used to attribute opinions. It indicates the origin of a piece of knowledge, a belief, information, an opinion, etc. It must always be followed by a subject pronoun:

> Según una encuesta, los libros que más entretienen son los de ficción. *(According to a survey, fiction books are the most entertaining.)*
> Este ingeniero es imprescindible según la NASA. *(According to NASA, this engineer is indispensable.)*
> Según mi modesta opinión, te estás equivocando. *(In my humble opinion, you're making a mistake.)*

8.3.p. *Sin*

The preposition *sin* expresses the lack or shortage of something, either physical or abstract:

> Hay organizaciones que atienden a personas sin hogar. *(There are organizations that help people without homes.)*
> Los misterios sin resolver atraen a los curiosos. *(Unsolved mysteries appeal to inquisitive people.)*
> Las aceitunas sin hueso son mejores para los niños pequeños. *(Olives without stones are better for small children.)*
> Payasos sin fronteras. *(Clowns without borders.)*

8.3.q. *Sobre*

The preposition *sobre* can be used in a variety of ways. Some of them reflect its literal meaning ('on', 'over' and 'above') and others do not.

The most common uses of *sobre* are:

- It indicates the position or location of something or somebody above or on another thing:

> El avión volaba sobre la ciudad. *(The plane flew over the city.)*
> Juega a hockey sobre hielo. *(He plays ice hockey.)*
> La casa está sobre el acantilado. *(The house is on the cliff.)*
> Estamos a mil metros sobre el nivel del mar. *(We're a thousand meters above sea level.)*

- It indicates an approximate number, time or amount:

> Busca un apartamento sobre los 300.000 dólares. *(He's looking for an apartment costing around 300,000 dollars.)*

PREP

8. Prepositions

Llegaré a cenar sobre las diez. *(I'll arrive for dinner around ten.)*

- It introduces the topic or subject of a text, conversation, speech, etc.:

Ya se ha publicado el último informe sobre el desempleo en el mundo. *(They've already published the latest report about unemployment around the world.)*
Este libro contiene todo lo que desee saber sobre mascotas. *(This book contains everything you want to know about pets.)*

8.3.r. *Tras*

The preposition *tras* is not particularly common in Spanish and is mainly used in more formal language. It is equivalent to *detrás de* and *después de*, which are used more often in spoken and written Spanish.

- It refers to the position of something behind another. In this case, *detrás de* can be used instead:

Los actores esperaban los aplausos tras el telón. *(The actors waited for the applause behind the curtain.)*
El sol se ocultó tras las montañas. *(The sun disappeared behind the mountains.)*

- It indicates an action taking place following an event. In this case, *después de* can be used instead:

Desalojaron una playa tras avistarse un tiburón azul. *(They cleared the beach after a blue shark was sighted.)*
Veinte jóvenes tuvieron que ser atendidos tras el accidente. *(Twenty young people needed medical assistance after the accident.)*

8.4. Prepositions governed by verbs (*preposiciones regidas*)

The use of one preposition or another is often determined by the verb. In fact, some verbs are followed by a specific preposition. For example, the verb *acordarse* must take an object introduced by *de*, the verb *confiar* requires *en* and the verb *pelearse* must take *con*. In these cases, the use of this preposition does not depend on its meaning but on the verb it is used with.

The verbs that require a specific preposition are called *verbos de régimen* in Spanish. The preposition they take is known as the *preposición regida*. Spanish has many verbs of this type.

The following is a reference list of the most common ones:

acordarse **de** algo	*to remember something*
acostumbrarse **a**	*to become accustomed **to**, to get used **to***
alegrarse **de** / **por**	*to be pleased **that**, to be glad **that***
arrepentirse **de**	*to be sorry **about**, to regret*
asustarse **de**	*to be frightened **of** / **by***
cansarse **de**	*to get tired **of***
confiar **en**	*to trust **in**, to rely **on***
disfrutar **de** / **con**	*to enjoy*
enfrentarse **a** / **con**	*to confront, to clash **with***
esforzarse **por**	*to strive **to**, to make an effort **to***
fijarse **en**	*to notice, to pay attention **to***
hablar **de** / **sobre**	*to talk **about***
interesarse **por**	*to take an interest **in***
intervenir **en** algo	*to take part **in** something*
invitar **a**	*to invite **to***
luchar **con**	*to fight **with***
luchar **contra**	*to fight **against***
negarse **a**	*to refuse **to***
olvidarse **de** algo	*to forget*
oponerse **a**	*to oppose, to be opposed to*
pensar **en** / **sobre**	*to think **about***
quejarse **de** / **por**	*to complain **about***
reírse **de**	*to laugh **at***
soñar **con** / **en**	*to dream **about** / **of***
sorprenderse **de**	*to be surprised **at***

PREP

9. Conjunctions

Conjunctions are words that connect parts of a sentence:

Me encontré a Ernesto y estuve hablando con él. *(I met Ernesto and had a chat with him.)*
Vi a Javier y a su hermano. *(I saw Javier and his brother.)*

Conjunctions are a closed class of words. In other words, they cannot be added to. They are always unstressed and never inflected.

Conjunctions are divided into two large groups: coordinating conjunctions and subordinating conjunctions.

● **Coordinating** conjunctions join single words or groups of words that have the same grammatical function (subject + subject, verb phrase + verb phrase, etc.):

Juan y Carlos *(Juan and Carlos)*
Habla despacio, pero aún así no lo entiendo. *(He speaks slowly, but I still can't understand him.)*

● **Subordinate** conjunctions are used to form subordinate clauses:

No sé si vendrá. *(I don't know if he'll come.)*
Dijo que no vendría. *(He said that he wouldn't come.)*

9.1. Coordinating conjunctions

Coordinating conjunctions establish a link between words or parts of a sentence that have the same grammatical function. They can be classified into three groups, according to the relationship they express:

Type	Meaning	Conjunctions
Copulative	They indicate addition	y (and its variant e), ni
Disjunctive	They link alternatives	o (and its variant u)
Adversative	They indicate total or partial opposition or contrast	pero, sino

9.1.a. Copulative coordinating conjunctions: *y, e, ni*

Copulative conjunctions basically indicate an addition or consequence. These conjunctions are used to connect words or parts of a sentence.

Use of *y*

The conjunction *y* allows us to connect a word, phrase or a clause to another. Both elements have the same grammatical function and normally express similar ideas or ideas that are interconnected:

Sergio y Luis estudiaron juntos. *(Sergio and Luis studied together.)*
Me gusta comer fruta y verdura. *(I like fruit and vegetables.)*

When linking more than one element, the conjunction is placed in front of the last element in the list:

Para preparar la ensalada necesito lechuga, tomate, cebolla y pimiento. *(I need lettuce, tomato, onion and pepper to make the salad.)*
Ve a casa, busca las llaves y vuelve. *(Go home, get the keys and come back.)*

In certain cases, the copulative conjunction *y* acquires different shades of meaning in addition to being a simple linking element. For instance, it can indicate:

- Condition:

   Hazle caso y vivirás feliz. *(Take notice of him and you'll be happy.)*

- Consequence:

   He estudiado mucho y sé más que tú. *(I've studied a lot and I know more than you.)*

- To indicate a contrast in ideas (adversative nuance):

   Sabía su dirección y ahora no me acuerdo. *(I knew his address and now I can't remember it.)*

Use of *e*

The copulative conjunction *y* changes to *e* when it precedes words that begin with *i-* or *hi-*:

Madre e hija conocen bien la historia del lugar. *(Mother and daughter know the history of the place well.)*
María e Inés son amigas desde la infancia. *(María and Inés have been friends since childhood.)*

CONJ

This rule does not apply to words beginning with *hie-*: *carbón y hierro (coal and iron.)*

Use of *ni*

When connecting negative clauses, or elements within a negative sentence, the conjunction *ni* is used instead of *y*:

No me gusta la blusa ni el pantalón. *(I don't like the blouse or the pants.)*
No juega limpio ni dice la verdad. *(He doesn't play fair or tell the truth.)*

Generally speaking, the conjunction *ni* is only used in front of the second element it connects. However, when the elements it connects precede the verb, or more than two elements are connected, we use *ni* in front of each of the elements:

Ni Susana ni Laura habían aprobado el curso. *(Neither Susana nor Laura passed their end-of-year exams.)*
No quiero discutir ni con Ana, ni con Patricia, ni con Luis. *(I don't want to argue with Ana, or Patricia, or Luis.)*

In other cases, it is not necessary to repeat *ni*. However, if we want to give added emphasis to the negation, *ni* can be placed in front of the first element.

- When connecting clauses, the first clause can be negated using *no*, but *ni* can also be used:

  Ni juega limpio ni dice la verdad. *(He neither plays fair nor tells the truth.)*

- When it connects words or phrases, *ni* can be placed in front of two negative elements linked by the conjunction:

  No lo hizo ni bien ni mal. *(He did it neither well nor badly.)*
  No es ni negro ni blanco. *(It's neither black nor white.)*

9.1.b. Disjunctive coordinating conjunctions: *o, u*

Disjunctive conjunctions are used to express a combination of alternatives. The most common disjunctive conjunction is *o*, although other possibilities exist that we will not deal with here as they correspond to a higher level of Spanish.

Use of *o*

The conjunction *o* is the most widely used disjunctive conjunction. It connects elements of the same level, indicates alternatives and the possibility of choosing between the two elements that are being expressed:

¿Tomarán vino blanco o vino tinto? *(Would you like white wine or red wine?)*
¿Quieres ir en autobús o en taxi? *(Do you want to go by bus or by taxi?)*

As a rule, the conjunction *o* is only placed in front of the second element. However, it can sometimes be placed in front of the first element. In these cases, both elements are mutually exclusive; that is, one possibility excludes the other:

O vienes o nos vamos sin ti. *(You either come or we'll leave without you.)*
O mi marido o yo asistiremos a la fiesta. *(Either my husband or I will come to the party.)*

O can also have other shades of meaning:

● It can indicate two options that are not incompatible:

Esta pintura puede usarse para interiores o para exteriores. *(This paint can be used for interiors or exteriors.)*

● Placed between two numbers, it indicates an approximate amount:

Pesa cincuenta o cincuenta y dos quilos. *(It weighs fifty or fifty-two kilos.)*

Use of *u*

The copulative conjunction *o* changes to *u* when it precedes words that begin with *o-* or *ho-*:

Quedó séptimo u octavo en la competición. *(He came seventh or eighth in the competition.)*
No sé si es belga u holandés. *(I don't know if he's Belgian or Dutch.)*

9.1.c. Adversative coordinating conjunctions

Adversative coordinating conjunctions connect parts of a sentence that express opposing or contrasting ideas. The opposition or contrast can be partial or total:

● Partial opposition:

Es simpático pero algo pelma. *(He's nice but a bit of a bore.)*

CONJ

9. Conjunctions

● Total opposition:

No lo dijo él sino yo. *(He didn't say it, I did.)*

The most widely used adversative conjunctions in Spanish are *pero* and *sino*. There are others, such as *mas*, but they correspond to a more advanced level of Spanish so we will not deal with them here.

The same notion of opposition between ideas can also be expressed by a series of linking expressions such as *sin embargo, no obstante, antes bien, con todo*, etc.

Use of *pero*

Pero is the most widely used adversative conjunction in Spanish. It is mainly used to express the partial contrast between ideas. The contrast can be between what has been said or what is deduced from what has been said:

Está nublado pero iremos a la playa igualmente. *(It's cloudy but we're going to the beach anyway.)*
La sopa está muy salada pero me gusta. *(The soup is very salty but I like it.)*
Parece increíble pero es cierto. *(It seems incredible but it's true.)*

The clause or part of the sentence introduced by *pero* go at the end. In other words, they can never be placed before the other coordinate element.

Use of *sino*

When the part of the sentence preceding the conjunction is negative and the part of the sentence following the conjunction is affirmative, we use *sino* instead of *pero*. In other words, *sino* introduces a statement that contradicts what was negated in the first part of the sentence.

No ha venido Teresa sino su hermano. *(Teresa didn't come, (but) her brother came instead.)*
No cambió el examen porque ella quisiera sino porque se lo pidió el director. *(She didn't put off the exam because she wanted to, but because the principal asked her to.)*
Compartir tus ideas no es malo sino todo lo contrario. *(It isn't bad to share your ideas, quite the opposite in fact.)*

As with *pero*, the element introduced by *sino* must come second in the sentence. In other words, it cannot precede the other coordinate element (the negative part of the sentence).

When connecting two conjugated verbs, *sino* is usually replaced with *sino que*:

No vino a verme sino que me llamó. *(He didn't come to see me, (but) he phoned instead.)*

9.2. Subordinating conjunctions

Subordinating conjunctions are used to introduce subordinate clauses. They are used to establish the relationship between the subordinate clause and the rest of the sentence.

They can be split into two large groups.

- The first consists of the conjunctions that introduce noun clauses: *que* and *si*.

- The second is formed by conjunctions that introduce subordinate clauses that express logical notions of causes, consequence, purpose, etc. They are classified according to the relationship between the subordinate clauses and the main clause in the following groups:

Type of clause	Conjunctions
Causal *They indicate cause*	porque, como que, dado que, pues, puesto que, ya que, etc.
Consecutive *They indicate consequence*	por (lo) tanto, así que, por consiguiente, luego, conque, por ello, así pues, de modo que, de manera que, etc.
Final *They express purpose or intention*	para que, a fin de que, a que, etc.
Conditional *They express the condition that is necessary for an action to be fulfilled*	si, a condición (de) que, con solo que, en caso (de) que, siempre que, etc.
Concessive *They express a circumstance that is expected to prevent an action from taking place but does not*	aunque, por más que, a pesar (de) que, pese a que, si bien, etc.

CONJ

One of the difficulties in using subordinate clauses is choosing the right verbal form: indicative, subjunctive or infinitive. However, we will not deal with this aspect here as it corresponds to a more advanced level of Spanish.

9.2.a. Noun conjunctions

They introduce subordinate clauses that perform the same function as a noun or can be replaced with *algo*:

> Sólo sabemos que llegará mañana. *(All we know is that he's going to arrive to-morrow.)*
> Están empeñados en que vayamos a su casa. *(They are determined that we should go to their house.)*
> Es necesario que vaya al médico. *(He needs to go to the doctor's.)*
> Quiero que vengas conmigo a Suiza. *(I want you to come with me to Switzerland.)*

The most widely used noun conjunction is *que*. The conjunction *si* is used to introduce subordinate clauses in an interrogative sense when they depend on a verb of communication (*decir, preguntar,* etc.) or a verb of knowledge (*saber, ignorar, conocer,* etc.):

> No sé si acompañaros o quedarme en casa. *(I don't know whether to come with you or stay home.)*
> Pregúntale si quiere más. *(Ask him if he wants any more.)*

9.2.b. Causal subordinate conjunctions

They introduce subordinate clauses that express the cause of, or give an explanation for what is being said in the main clause. The most common causal conjunction is *porque*:

> Canta en una coral porque le gusta. *(He sings in a choir because he likes it.)*
> Está triste porque no ha ganado. *(He's sad because he didn't win.)*
> Vine porque se lo prometí. *(I came because I promised to.)*

There are other causal conjunctions in Spanish as well as *porque*:

> Como hizo mal tiempo, no fuimos a la playa. *(As the weather was bad, we didn't go to the beach.)*
> Dado que la ley lo contempla, podemos presentar recurso. *(Given that the law allows it, we can appeal.)*
> Aceptó la oferta puesto que no había otra solución. *(He accepted the offer because there was no other solution.)*
> Se lo contaré yo, ya que es culpa mía. *(I'll tell him since it was my fault.)*

9.2.c. Consecutive subordinate conjunctions

They introduce subordinate clauses that express a conclusion to, or the consequence of what is being said in the main clause. The most common consecutive conjunctions are *por (lo) tanto*, *por consiguiente* and *así que*. The first two are often combined with the conjunction *y*:

> Estamos de fiesta y, por (lo) tanto, alegres. *(We're having a party, so we're happy.)*
> No tiene los permisos del ayuntamiento y por consiguiente no puede abrir el local. *(He doesn't have the permits from the council and therefore he can't open the bar.)*
> Tienen sueño, así que se van a la cama. *(They're tired, so they're going to bed.)*

9.2.d. Final subordinating conjunctions

They introduce subordinate clauses that express the purpose, intention or objective of the action being expressed in the main clause. The most common is *para que*:

> Está haciendo lo imposible para que su hermana pueda regresar. *(He's doing everything he can so that his sister can come back.)*
> Piden precaución en la carretera para que no se repita un accidente como éste. *(They're asking people to be careful on the roads so that an accident like this won't happen again.)*
> Unieron esfuerzos para que sus derechos se respetaran. *(They all joined forces so that their rights would be respected.)*

The conjunction *a fin de que* is often used and is interchangeable with *para que*, although it is more formal.

9.2.e. Conditional subordinate conjunctions

They introduce subordinate clauses that specify the conditions that are necessary for the action in the main clause to be fulfilled. The most widely used conditional conjunction is *si*:

> Dejaré de trabajar si me toca la lotería. *(I would stop working if I won the lottery.)*
> Si al final viene, te iremos a buscar los dos. *(If he turns up, we'll come and get you both.)*
> Si ves a tu hermana, dale de recuerdos de mi parte. *(If you see your sister, give her my regards.)*

9.2.f. Concessive subordinate conjunctions

They introduce subordinate clauses that express a circumstance that is expected to prevent an action from taking place but does not. The most widely used concessive conjunction is *aunque*:

CONJ

9. Conjunctions

Aunque no haga sol iremos a la playa. (*Even if it's not sunny, we'll go to the beach.*)

Vale la pena arriesgarse aunque estés perdiendo. (*It's worth taking a risk although you're losing.*)

Aunque me duela, me operaré este año. (*Although it might hurt, I'm going to have the operation this year.*)

There are other conjunctions as well. For example:

Por más que busco, no encuentro nada. (*No matter how much I look, I can't find anything.*)

La obesidad crece pese a que la población hace más ejercicio. (*Obesity is on the increase despite the fact that people are doing more exercise.*)

No he logrado entenderlo a pesar de que me lo ha explicado varias veces. (*I can't quite grasp it although you've told me several times.*)